DAMN
delicious

DAMN delicious

100 SUPER EASY, SUPER FAST RECIPES

CHUNGAH RHEE

Oxmoor House®

Published by Oxmoor House, an imprint of Time Inc. Books
225 Liberty Street, New York, NY 10281

Senior Editor: Betty Wong
Project Editor: Lacie Pinyan
Senior Designer: Maribeth Jones
Junior Designer: Olivia Pierce
Recipe Testers: Callie Nash, Julia Levy, Karen Rankin
Assistant Production Manager: Diane Rose Keener
Associate Project Manager: Hillary Leary
Copy Editors: Jacqueline Giovanelli, Sarah Scheffel
Proofreaders: Adrienne Davis, Julie Gillis
Indexer: Mary Ann Laurens
Fellow: Mallory Short

Additional nutrition tips by Jessica Penner, RD at Smart Nutrition

Additional photography:
front cover, pages 13, 58 (top center), 79, 98, 104, 136 (bottom center),
171, 172 (top center), 206 (top right), 233 (right): ©Trever Hoehne,
creative direction: Nick Hounslow; pages 5, 8 (left), 40 (top right), 92 (top
center), 100, 116 (bottom left), 122, 219, 223 (left): ©Thayer Allison Gowdy;
pages 10, 85, 206 (bottom right), 225: Iain Bagwell

ISBN-13: 978-0-8487-4585-1
ISBN-10: 0-8487-4585-X
Library of Congress Control Number: 2016942854

First Edition 2016

Printed in the United States of America

10 9 8 7 6 5 4 3 2 1

Time Inc. Books products may be purchased for business or promotional use.
For information on bulk purchases, please contact Christi Crowley in the
Special Sales Department at (845) 895-9858.

We welcome your comments and suggestions about Time Inc. Books.
Please write to us at:

Time Inc. Books
Attention: Book Editors
P.O. Box 62310
Tampa, Florida 33662-2310

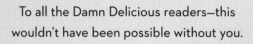

To all the Damn Delicious readers—this
wouldn't have been possible without you.

CONTENTS

INTRODUCTION

I used to think I was too busy, too tired, and too uninspired to cook a delicious and exciting meal every night. I bet you think that, too. But I'm going to show you that, no matter how busy or hectic life gets, there's always time to put dinner on the table. Forget the days when dinner was an hour-long fiasco of failed recipes and dishes piled in the sink—a healthy and delicious meal can be done in just 20 to 30 minutes from start to finish. That's what this cookbook is all about—helping people just like you, who don't have any time to spare during the week, get back in the kitchen and whip up satisfying meals without all the fuss.

When we're short on time, we typically sacrifice a home-cooked meal. After all, who has the time to create dinner from scratch when we still need to walk the dog, help the kids with homework, and catch up on e-mail? That usually leaves us resorting to frozen dinners, delivery, or drive-through meals to feed ourselves. But these options can quickly become a strain on our wallets and our waistlines.

That's the scenario that inspired me to create my blog, Damn Delicious, with the goal of developing super-easy recipes as a way to eat healthier and lose weight. I had just gained 30 pounds during my last year of college, and yet I continued to eat out for every single meal while studying and applying to grad school. I habitually told myself, "There's just not enough time to cook," as I ordered Chinese takeout or pulled into the drive-through at In-N-Out. But eventually, I got back into the kitchen, where I began to discover cooking shortcuts and easy ways to prepare satisfying, nutritious meals that were actually skinny-jeans friendly. I also saved a ton of money by cooking at home, especially when I learned how to create dishes using affordable pantry ingredients and repurposing leftovers.

After years of documenting my experiments in quick, low-fuss cooking on my blog, I've watched Damn Delicious grow into a vibrant community of cooks from around the world. My readers often tell me they love the simplicity of my recipes, swearing that even the picky eaters in their households gobble up every last bite! I also love hearing from readers who are just beginning to cook and who seem relieved that my recipes are not only unintimidating, but work every time and involve minimal cleanup. (I'm all about doing fewer dishes.)

When I saw how my recipes were helping readers bring fun and ease into their cooking routines, I knew I wanted to do something more. That's why I decided to write this book. By sharing the recipes collected here, I hope to make cooking at home even more effortless for my regular readers, while also inspiring and encouraging a whole new set of cooks. I've always dreamed of a pretty, go-to cookbook that you can flip through when you need inspiration and motivation to skip the drive-through lane and make an amazing homemade meal instead. I hope that this book will serve that purpose for you, and that eventually, you'll start to reach for it instead of the stack of takeout menus. I want you to feel confident and creative in the kitchen. I truly believe that, just by getting back into the kitchen, even a few days a week, a healthy lifestyle change can happen, just as it did for me.

In this book you'll find more than 100 recipes, all of them delicious, foolproof, and a cinch to throw together. They include both brand-new, exciting ideas and some of the best tried-and-true classics that the readers of my blog love most. This cookbook is designed to be your one-stop shop for everything from fast breakfasts, one-pot wonders, quickie takeout copycats, skinny favorites, superfast dinners, and even insanely easy drinks and desserts. I've also included some of my favorite go-to dishes, such as zero cleanup foil packets (pages 160, 163) and healthy zoodle (a.k.a. zucchini noodle) recipes (pages 105, 106). Along with my tips for easy meal prep and speedy grocery shopping, you'll find that cooking dinner has never been easier!

So get ready to revive and rethink your mealtime routine. I hope you'll realize that, with just the right recipes and strategies, you can put the fun—and the yum—back into cooking!

STRATEGIES, SHORTCUTS & SOLUTIONS
to Get More Yum in Less Time

SHOP SMARTER FOR SPEEDY COOKING

Knowing what to stock up on and what you can store in the fridge guarantees you can always fix up something delicious (and affordable) in just minutes. Here are the essentials I always keep on hand.

Frozen vegetables and fruit are super convenient and ensure you can have your favorites all year. They're prewashed, pre-chopped, and pre-packaged! I always have frozen broccoli, carrots, corn, green beans, peas, and spinach on hand. Frozen strawberries, blueberries, mango chunks, and peaches also come in handy for quick breakfast smoothies and muffins.

Frozen shrimp can be kept for up to 2 months and are a great staple for fast weeknight cooking. The best way to thaw shrimp is to let them sit overnight in the fridge. But if you're in a rush, you can place the shrimp in a colander and run them under cold water for about 10 minutes.

Chicken breasts can be stored in the freezer for about 6 months. Wrap them and repack in freezer bags instead of leaving them in the store packaging. Thaw frozen chicken overnight in the refrigerator.

Ground beef is another freezer-friendly staple. Buy in bulk, but freeze it in small portions so you can thaw it more quickly when you need it.

Greek yogurt is one of my go-to ingredients. It is an amazing substitute for many high-fat ingredients like mayonnaise, sour cream, or cream cheese. And often you can't taste the difference. I promise!

Dried pasta will last on your shelf for a couple of years. I reach for spaghetti, fettucine, linguine, and macaroni again and again, even to make some of my Asian-inspired dishes.

Canned black beans, kidney beans, corn, and crushed and diced tomatoes are very versatile. Stock up when they're on sale.

Dijon mustard, honey, rice wine vinegar, white wine vinegar, reduced-sodium soy sauce, and Sriracha are my pantry essentials.

Quinoa and rice (both white and brown) play supporting roles in many of my meals.

Dried vs. Fresh Herbs Yes, fresh herbs are great, but unless you're making something like pesto that absolutely requires fresh basil leaves, you can always use dried herbs. Just keep this ratio in mind: fresh herbs to dry is 3:1.

BUY IT FRESH

I recommend purchasing organic apples, pears, strawberries, peaches, sweet bell peppers, celery, spinach, lettuce, potatoes, and carrots, to name a few, as they are the most susceptible to pesticide residue.

I also always suggest using freshly grated Parmesan cheese above anything else. There is a noticeable taste difference between fresh Parmesan and the kind that comes in the green can.

MAKE EXTRA

When you cook grains, make a large batch. As you'll notice in the book, I often use leftover rice or quinoa. Cooked rice and grains can keep in the refrigerator for a few days or frozen for a couple of months. You can use cold quinoa the next day in breakfast bowls (page 23), or use leftover rice in Kimchi Fried Rice (page 73), Beef and Broccoli Bowls (page 82), or California Roll Bowls (page 88).

You should also make extra of the sauces, salad dressings, soups, smoothies, and dips in this book to give yourself a headstart on prepping other meals throughout the week.

How to Cook Quinoa

Cooking perfectly delicate and fluffy quinoa is actually quite easy: All you need is a ratio of 1 cup uncooked quinoa to 2 cups liquid—it can be water, chicken broth, or vegetable broth—it's up to you. Let it come to boil, reduce heat to low, cover, and simmer until the liquid has been absorbed, about 20 minutes. Fluff with a fork. But the most important thing to remember is to thoroughly rinse the quinoa before cooking using a fine mesh strainer—this will help remove any bitterness.

CAN I COOK IT IN A SLOW COOKER?

Damn Delicious readers always love a good slow cooker recipe, so I included an entire chapter devoted to that. Here are just a few tips to make sure you get good results: Although there are a range of slow cooker sizes, I find that the 5- to 6-quart slow cooker is the best for my recipes. Fill it up only ⅔ of the way. Your slow cooker shouldn't be overcrowded. To prevent any food-safety issues, be sure all meats and vegetables are fully thawed before adding them to your slow cooker. If time permits, I recommend browning your meat before adding it to the cooker. Yes, it's an extra step, but it adds a layer of rich caramelized goodness. (And don't forget the browned bits in the pan—they're absolute gold.) Add dairy products in at the very end of cooking to avoid curdling. And as a general rule of thumb, the low setting will cook twice as long as the high setting. However, temperature settings can vary with different models, so make notes on what works for yours and adjust your cook time if necessary.

WHAT IS A SPIRAL VEGETABLE SLICER OR SPIRALIZER?

A spiralizer is a hand-operated kitchen tool or machine that creates vegetable "noodles" in seconds. It's an affordable investment that's a simple and easy way to sneak in extra veggies or add a new texture to pastas and salads. You can use it with many fruits and vegetables, including cucumbers, carrots, zucchini, and even apples. I use it in several recipes like the Zucchini Lo Mein (page 105) and Zucchini Salad with Roasted Tomatoes and Mozzarella (page 106).

RECIPE KEY

GF = gluten free

KF = kid friendly

VEG = vegetarian

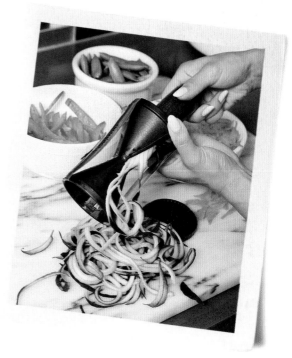

The cinnamon-cream cheese glaze is everything.

Make a double batch to freeze.

1
PUT THE FAST INTO BREAKFAST

Breakfast is the most important meal of the day, right? But chances are there are plenty of mornings when you barely have time to get a pot of coffee going. That's where these recipes come in, making it easy to get a good-for-you meal done even when you're on the go.

The best part about a smoothie in a bowl is how customizable it is. Add toppings like fresh berries, almonds, and your cereal of choice—I like my childhood fave Cap'n Crunch, but Fruity Pebbles or Cheerios are also good additions. Finish the bowl off with a yogurt drizzle to add a little bit of pizazz to your breakfast. It's like a delicious AM dessert, but nutritious!

STRAWBERRY and CREAM SMOOTHIE BOWL

SERVES 2   PREP TIME: 10 MINUTES   TOTAL TIME: 10 MINUTES   KF VEG

1 (10-ounce) package frozen whole strawberries (see Note)

1 cup vanilla Greek yogurt, plus more for topping

½ cup milk

2 tablespoons old-fashioned oats

¼ cup nuts, cereal, berries, or other fruit, for topping, optional

1. In a blender, combine strawberries, Greek yogurt, milk, and oats and puree until smooth.

2. Top with additional berries, fruit, nuts, or cereal, if desired.

3. Serve immediately, drizzled with additional yogurt.

Note: Frozen blueberries or raspberries can be substituted for the frozen strawberries.

PER SERVING: CALORIES 217 FAT 11.3g PROTEIN 9g CARB 21g FIBER 4g CHOL 40mg IRON 1mg SODIUM 81mg CALC 198mg

TIP

When eaten at breakfast, Greek yogurt's high-protein content can help curb afternoon snack cravings!

I was so hungry one morning that I ran into a local coffee shop to grab a granola berry parfait to scarf down. I was really excited about it, except it cost $9.95. For yogurt. With two spoonfuls of granola. And like four berries.

So, now I make these berry parfaits at home. And because they can be assembled in handy to-go containers two days ahead, there's no reason to ever go hungry (or spend too much) during those busy mornings. Each serving costs less than $3, and you get more than four berries, too.

MAKE-AHEAD GRANOLA BERRY PARFAIT

SERVES 1   PREP TIME: 10 MINUTES   TOTAL TIME: 10 MINUTES   KF VEG

½ cup plain Greek yogurt

1 tablespoon honey

½ vanilla bean, seeds scraped and reserved

¼ cup hulled and quartered fresh strawberries

¼ cup fresh blueberries

¼ cup granola

1. In a small bowl, whisk together the yogurt, honey, and vanilla bean seeds.

2. Using a mason jar or another small jar, layer the yogurt mixture, strawberries, blueberries, and granola.

3. Screw on the lid, and refrigerate for up to 2 days.

PER SERVING: CALORIES 287 FAT 6.1g PROTEIN 13g CARB 50g FIBER 3g CHOL 15mg IRON 1mg SODIUM 102mg CALC 142mg

TIP

If serving immediately, repeat the yogurt-berry-granola layers for a pretty presentation. If you are making parfaits for later, it is best to keep the granola on top of the berries to keep it from getting soggy.

Good for you? Sure. Delicious? Absolutely. This smoothie is chock-full of greens, berries, and oats to keep you full and refreshed.

BERRY GREEN SMOOTHIE

SERVES 2   **PREP TIME:** 5 MINUTES   **TOTAL TIME:** 5 MINUTES   VEG

1 cup loosely packed spinach leaves

½ cup frozen blueberries

½ cup frozen raspberries

1 ripe banana

½ cup milk, almond milk, or soy milk

2 tablespoons old-fashioned oats

1 tablespoon sugar, or more to taste

In a blender, combine the spinach, blueberries, raspberries, banana, milk, oats, sugar, and 1 cup ice, and puree until smooth. Serve immediately.

PER SERVING: CALORIES 172 **FAT** 3g **PROTEIN** 4g **CARB** 35g **FIBER** 6g **CHOL** 8mg **IRON** 2mg **SODIUM** 53mg **CALC** 120mg

The avocado makes this smoothie creamy and packs it full of healthy fats and potassium. For even easier prep, you can freeze individual portions of the fruits and veggies, and then just add in the milk and pineapple juice when you're ready to blend!

PINEAPPLE, AVOCADO, and KALE SMOOTHIE

SERVES 3   **PREP TIME:** 5 MINUTES   **TOTAL TIME:** 5 MINUTES   GF VEG

3 cups loosely packed baby kale

1 ripe avocado, halved, seeded, and peeled

1 apple, cored and chopped

1 ripe banana

1 cup chopped pineapple

1 cup milk, almond milk, or soy milk

½ cup pineapple juice

In a high-powered blender, combine the kale, avocado, apple, banana, pineapple, milk, pineapple juice, and 1 cup ice, and puree until smooth. Serve immediately.

PER SERVING: CALORIES 257 **FAT** 10.5g **PROTEIN** 5g **CARB** 40g **FIBER** 8g **CHOL** 10mg **IRON** 1mg **SODIUM** 59mg **CALC** 219mg

If you have leftover quinoa from the night before, you can reuse it in these easy and nutritious breakfast bowls. I prefer to eat my quinoa bowl at room temperature, but this is also really good served warm. Add any of your favorite fruit, such as mango and pineapple for a tropical twist, or try strawberries, blackberries, and blueberries for a fully loaded berry bowl—the combinations are endless!

QUINOA BREAKFAST BOWLS

SERVES 4   **PREP TIME:** 5 MINUTES   **TOTAL TIME:** 5 MINUTES   `GF` `KF` `VEG`

1 ⅓ to 2 cups vanilla soy milk or almond milk

¼ teaspoon ground cinnamon

1 vanilla bean, split in half lengthwise, seeds scraped and reserved

2 cups cooked quinoa

¼ cup fresh blueberries

¼ cup fresh raspberries

1 ripe banana, thinly sliced

1 kiwi, peeled and diced

1 tablespoon honey, optional

1. In a large glass measuring cup, whisk together the soy milk, cinnamon, and vanilla bean seeds.

2. Spoon the quinoa evenly into serving bowls. Stir in the milk mixture.

3. Serve immediately, topped with the blueberries, raspberries, banana, kiwi, and a drizzle of honey, if desired.

PER SERVING: CALORIES 238 **FAT** 4.6g **PROTEIN** 9g **CARB** 41g **FIBER** 6g **CHOL** 0mg **IRON** 4mg **SODIUM** 84mg **CALC** 141mg

TIP

Quinoa is a good replacement for oats, as it contains roughly the same amount of key nutrients such as protein, fiber, and magnesium.

Who wouldn't want a complete breakfast that comes together in just 25 minutes? This one lets you combine everything into ramekins and pop them into the oven while you get ready for your day. You can also easily double or triple this recipe for weekend company. They'll be so impressed, they won't know what hit them.

SPICY MARINARA BAKED EGGS

SERVES 4   PREP TIME: 5 MINUTES   TOTAL TIME: 25 MINUTES

1 cup marinara sauce

½ teaspoon crushed red pepper flakes (see Note)

½ teaspoon dried basil

½ teaspoon dried oregano

8 large eggs

½ cup shredded mozzarella cheese

¼ cup freshly grated Parmesan cheese

Kosher salt and freshly ground black pepper, to taste

2 tablespoons chopped fresh parsley leaves, for garnish, optional

1. Preheat the oven to 425°F. Lightly oil four 10-ounce ramekins or coat them with nonstick spray.

2. In a large bowl, whisk together the marinara sauce, red pepper flakes, basil, and oregano.

3. Add ¼ cup of the marinara sauce mixture to each prepared ramekin. Top each with 2 eggs (be careful not to break the yolks), 2 tablespoons mozzarella, and 1 tablespoon Parmesan; season with salt and pepper to taste.

4. Bake until the egg whites are cooked through, 15 to 20 minutes, or until desired doneness.

5. Serve immediately in the ramekins, garnished with parsley, if desired.

Note: The crushed red pepper can be omitted completely for a nonspicy version.

PER SERVING: CALORIES 293 FAT 18.7g PROTEIN 23g CARB 7g FIBER 1g CHOL 391mg IRON 2mg SODIUM 885mg CALC 380mg

This baked egg dish makes for a simple, elegant breakfast—perfect for brunch. The savory veggies serve as a colorful bed for the eggs, and you can add ham or bacon.

BAKED EGGS with KALE, TOMATOES, and MUSHROOMS

SERVES 4   PREP TIME: 7 MINUTES   TOTAL TIME: 24 MINUTES   GF

4 cups chopped kale leaves

1 pint cherry tomatoes (about 2 cups)

2 cups sliced cremini mushrooms

1 tablespoon olive oil

2 garlic cloves, minced

Kosher salt and freshly ground black pepper, to taste

4 large eggs

2 tablespoons freshly grated Parmesan cheese

1/2 teaspoon dried thyme

1/2 teaspoon dried oregano

1/2 teaspoon dried basil

1/4 teaspoon crushed red pepper flakes, or more to taste

Kosher salt and freshly ground black pepper, to taste

1. Preheat the oven to 400°F. Lightly oil a baking sheet or coat it with nonstick spray.

2. Arrange the kale, tomatoes, and mushrooms in a single layer on the prepared baking sheet. Add the olive oil and garlic, and season with salt and pepper to taste. Gently toss to combine, making sure to evenly distribute the tomatoes and mushrooms among the kale leaves.

3. Bake the vegetables for 8 to 10 minutes, until the tomatoes begin to blister. Remove the baking sheet from the oven.

4. Make the eggs: Divide the vegetables evenly into 4 mounds on the pan. Create a small well in the center of each mound. Gently crack 1 egg, and slide it into a well, keeping the yolk intact. Repeat with the remaining eggs.

5. In a small bowl, toss together the cheese, thyme, oregano, basil, and red pepper flakes; sprinkle evenly over each cracked egg, and season with salt and pepper to taste.

6. Return the pan to the oven, and continue to bake for 7 to 9 minutes, until the egg whites have set but the yolks are still runny. Using a spatula, gently transfer the mounds of veggies with eggs to plates, and serve immediately.

PER SERVING: CALORIES 162 FAT 10.5g PROTEIN 11g CARB 7g FIBER 2g CHOL 189mg IRON 2mg SODIUM 397mg CALC 204mg

Fresh guacamole and an easy blender hollandaise sauce give this eggs benedict breakfast a very California-style twist. You can take it a step further and add bacon or ham, or go more classic with Canadian bacon.

GUACAMOLE EGGS BENEDICT

SERVES 4   PREP TIME: 20 MINUTES   TOTAL TIME: 30 MINUTES

FOR THE GUACAMOLE

2 ripe avocados, halved, seeded, and peeled

¼ cup diced red onion

2 tablespoons chopped fresh cilantro leaves

Juice of 1 lime

Kosher salt and freshly ground black pepper, to taste

FOR THE HOLLANDAISE SAUCE

4 large egg yolks

1 tablespoon freshly squeezed lemon juice

1 teaspoon Sriracha sauce, optional

¼ teaspoon salt

6 tablespoons unsalted butter, melted

Kosher salt and freshly ground black pepper, to taste

4 large eggs

2 English muffins, split in half, toasted

2 Roma tomatoes, thinly sliced

2 tablespoons chopped fresh parsley leaves, for garnish, optional

1. Make the guacamole: Mash the avocados in a medium bowl using a potato masher or fork. Add red onion, cilantro, lime juice, salt and pepper to taste, and gently stir to combine. Set aside.

2. Make the hollandaise sauce: Combine the egg yolks, lemon juice, Sriracha, and salt in a blender until pale yellow in color, 30 to 60 seconds. With the motor running, add the butter in a slow stream until emulsified; season with salt and pepper (see Note).

3. In a small saucepan, bring 3 cups of water to a simmer over medium-high heat. Working one at a time, crack an egg into a small bowl, and slide it gently into the water; repeat with the remaining eggs, keeping distance between the eggs. Turn off the heat, and cover for 3 to 4 minutes, or until the whites are cooked and the yolks are still soft. Using a slotted spoon, remove the eggs, draining them well.

4. Spoon ¼ cup guacamole on each English muffin. Top with 1 tomato slice and poached egg, and drizzle with the hollandaise sauce.

5. Serve immediately, garnished with parsley, if desired.

Note: If the sauce is too thick, add lukewarm water, a teaspoon at a time, as needed until desired consistency is reached. Keep warm in a heatproof bowl set over hot water until ready to serve.

PER SERVING: CALORIES 483 FAT 38.4g PROTEIN 12g CARB 25g FIBER 6g CHOL 416mg IRON 3mg SODIUM 568mg CALC 115mg

Sometimes you want to dress up your French toast with more than just plain old maple syrup, and that's when you top it with a homemade blueberry sauce complete with a splash of Grand Marnier. Best of all, you can use either fresh or frozen blueberries in this sauce, so it's great all year long. (And hey, if you want an even more decadent French toast, go ahead and add a scoop of vanilla ice cream.)

FRENCH TOAST *with* BLUEBERRY ORANGE SAUCE

SERVES 4   PREP TIME: 10 MINUTES   TOTAL TIME: 25 MINUTES   VEG

FOR THE BLUEBERRY ORANGE SAUCE

1 tablespoon cornstarch

2 cups fresh or frozen blueberries

¼ cup sugar

2 tablespoons orange-flavored liqueur, such as Grand Marnier or Cointreau

3 large eggs

¾ cup milk

3 tablespoons sugar

½ teaspoon vanilla extract

¼ teaspoon ground cinnamon

Pinch of ground nutmeg

8 (¾-inch-thick) slices challah, brioche, or white bread

2 tablespoons unsalted butter

1. Make the blueberry orange sauce: Combine the cornstarch and 1 tablespoon water in a small bowl; set aside.

2. In a medium saucepan, combine the blueberries, sugar, and orange-flavored liqueur over medium-high heat. Stir in the cornstarch mixture. Bring to a boil; cook 1 minute, stirring constantly, until the sauce has thickened. Reduce the heat to low and keep warm.

3. Make the French toast: Whisk together the eggs, milk, sugar, vanilla, cinnamon, and nutmeg in a large bowl. Working one at a time, dip the bread slices into the egg mixture.

4. Melt 1 tablespoon butter in a large skillet over medium-high heat. Working in batches, add the bread slices to the skillet, two to three at a time, and cook until evenly golden brown, 1 to 2 minutes on each side. Reduce the heat to medium if the pan becomes too hot, and add butter as needed with each batch.

5. Serve immediately with warm blueberry orange sauce.

PER SERVING: CALORIES 554 FAT 14.9g PROTEIN 16g CARB 86g FIBER 2g CHOL 168mg IRON 4mg SODIUM 528mg CALC 85mg

Yes, this is a simple avocado toast fancied up with just a few ingredients: lemon zest, red pepper flakes, and freshly ground black pepper. What makes it extra special is the runny poached egg on top. Bacon can also be added for a complete breakfast. Just saying.

AVOCADO TOAST

SERVES 2   PREP TIME: 15 MINUTES   TOTAL TIME: 20 MINUTES   `KF` `VEG`

2 large eggs

2 slices bread, toasted (see Note)

1 avocado, peeled, seeded, and thinly sliced

2 teaspoons olive oil

¼ teaspoon crushed red pepper flakes

Kosher salt and freshly ground black pepper, to taste

1 tablespoon chopped fresh parsley leaves, for garnish, optional

1 tablespoon black sesame seeds, optional

Zest of 1 lemon, optional

1. In a small saucepan, bring 3 cups water to a simmer over medium-high heat. Working one at a time, crack an egg into a small bowl, and slide it gently into the water; repeat with the remaining egg, keeping distance between the two eggs. Turn off the heat, and cover for 3 to 4 minutes, or until the whites are cooked and the yolks are still soft. Using a slotted spoon, remove the eggs, draining them well.

2. Top the toasted bread with the avocado slices, and drizzle them with olive oil; sprinkle with the red pepper flakes. Season with salt and pepper to taste.

3. Serve the avocado toast immediately, topped with the poached eggs and garnished with parsley, sesame seeds, or lemon zest, if desired.

Note: Any type of bread can be used here, although you can't go wrong with freshly baked, thick, crusty artisan breads.

PER SERVING: CALORIES 317 FAT 21.5g PROTEIN 9g CARB 23g FIBER 6g CHOL 186mg IRON 2mg SODIUM 468mg CALC 31mg

TIP

This breakfast provides a good balance of macronutrients: complex carbs from the bread, healthy fats from the avocado, and protein from the eggs.

Re-imagine your favorite bagel and lox with these cute bite-sized toasts topped with whipped feta, thinly sliced smoked salmon, arugula, and capers. After all, finger foods just taste so much better, especially for breakfast! But be wary of its size. I ate about 10 of these before I realized there were only a few left for my guests. Oops.

MINI LOX TOAST

SERVES 6   PREP TIME: 20 MINUTES   TOTAL TIME: 25 MINUTES

FOR THE WHIPPED FETA

8 ounces crumbled feta cheese

4 ounces cream cheese, at room temperature

2 cloves garlic, peeled and left whole

Kosher salt and freshly ground black pepper, to taste

2 tablespoons olive oil

1 (16-ounce) sourdough loaf, cut into ¼-inch-thick slices

2 tablespoons olive oil

2 cups loosely packed arugula

3 ounces smoked salmon, thinly sliced

¼ cup thinly sliced red onion

2 tablespoons capers, drained

1. Make the whipped feta: Combine the feta cheese, cream cheese, and garlic in the bowl of a food processor, and pulse until the cheeses are whipped and the garlic is finely chopped; season with salt and pepper to taste. With the motor running, add the olive oil in a slow stream until emulsified.

2. Preheat the oven to 425°F.

3. Brush each slice of bread with olive oil. Put the bread on a baking sheet, and bake until crisp and lightly golden around the edges, 5 to 6 minutes.

4. Top each slice of toast with whipped feta, arugula, smoked salmon, red onion, and capers, dividing the toppings evenly. Serve immediately.

PER SERVING: CALORIES 486 FAT 26.6g PROTEIN 20g CARB 43g FIBER 2g CHOL 68mg IRON 4mg SODIUM 1145mg CALC 276mg

Skip the morning bakery run and whip up these muffins right at home—they're easier to make than you think, and you can load up on as many chocolate chips as you like. Or swap out the chocolate chips for blueberries, raspberries, blackberries, or strawberries. After you've stuffed your face with muffins straight out of the oven (be careful not to burn your tongue!), freeze the rest in individual servings for up to 2 months. Reheat in the microwave for 30 seconds.

BAKERY STYLE CHOCOLATE CHIP MUFFINS

MAKES 12 MUFFINS   **PREP TIME:** 10 MINUTES   **TOTAL TIME:** 27 MINUTES   KF   VEG

1 ³/₄ cups all-purpose flour

2 teaspoons baking powder

1 teaspoon baking soda

¹/₄ teaspoon salt

²/₃ cup granulated sugar

¹/₂ cup milk

4 tablespoons unsalted butter, melted

¹/₄ cup vegetable oil

2 large eggs

1 teaspoon vanilla extract

1 cup semi-sweet chocolate chips, or more if desired

2 tablespoons sparkling sugar

1. Preheat the oven to 375°F. Line a standard 12-cup muffin tin with paper liners; set aside.

2. In a large bowl, combine the flour, baking powder, baking soda, and salt.

3. In a large glass measuring cup or another bowl, whisk together the sugar, milk, melted butter, vegetable oil, eggs, and vanilla.

4. Pour the wet mixture over the dry ingredients, and stir using a rubber spatula just until moist. Add the chocolate chips, and gently toss to combine.

5. Spoon the batter into the prepared muffin tin, dividing it evenly. Sprinkle the tops with sparkling sugar. Bake for 15 to 17 minutes, or until a toothpick inserted in the center of a muffin comes out clean.

6. Cool on a wire rack before removing the muffins from the tin. Serve warm or at room temperature.

PER SERVING: CALORIES 279 **FAT** 14g **PROTEIN** 4g **CARB** 42g **FIBER** 1g **CHOL** 42mg **IRON** 1mg **SODIUM** 264mg **CALC** 42mg

This fun twist on a traditional French toast bake uses buttery, flaky mini croissants instead. Start this the night before to give the croissants a chance to soak up all of that sweet egg batter. To finish it off, drizzle the bread pudding–like goodness with cinnamon–cream cheese glaze. This recipe is a good way to use up day-old croissants, and you can also swap the blueberries for any other berry combo.

OVERNIGHT BLUEBERRY CROISSANT BREAKFAST BAKE

SERVES 4   PREP TIME: 15 MINUTES   TOTAL TIME: 55 MINUTES, PLUS CHILLING   `KF` `VEG`

10 mini croissants or 6 croissants, cut into 1-inch cubes

1 cup fresh or frozen blueberries

1 ½ cups milk

3 large eggs

2 tablespoons maple syrup, or more to taste

Zest of 1 lemon

1 ½ teaspoons vanilla extract

½ teaspoon ground cinnamon

¼ teaspoon ground nutmeg

FOR THE CINNAMON-CREAM CHEESE GLAZE

2 tablespoons cream cheese, at room temperature

¼ cup confectioners' sugar

2 tablespoons milk

¼ teaspoon ground cinnamon

1. Make the blueberry croissant bake: Lightly coat a 9- x 13-inch baking dish with nonstick spray. Arrange a layer of croissants evenly in the prepared baking dish; top with an even layer of blueberries.

2. In a large glass measuring cup or another bowl, whisk together the milk, eggs, maple syrup, lemon zest, vanilla, cinnamon, and nutmeg. Pour the mixture evenly over the croissants and blueberries. Cover the baking dish with plastic wrap, and place in the refrigerator for at least 2 hours or overnight.

3. When you're ready to bake, preheat the oven to 350°F.

4. Remove the plastic wrap from the pan, and bake for 35 to 40 minutes, or until golden brown.

5. Make the cinnamon-cream cheese glaze: Combine the cream cheese, confectioners' sugar, milk, and cinnamon in a small bowl, and stir until smooth.

6. Serve immediately, drizzled with the cinnamon-cream cheese glaze.

PER SERVING: CALORIES 468 FAT 24.2g PROTEIN 13g CARB 52g FIBER 2g CHOL 203mg IRON 3mg SODIUM 393mg CALC 168mg

This is made for one right from the microwave.

Made without heavy cream or cream cheese.

2

ONE-POT COMFORT IN 30 MINUTES

Create a balanced bowl of deliciousness without pulling out every piece of cookware in your kitchen. These recipes are perfect for anyone who wants to spend less time at the sink and more time on the rest of their life.

This Alfredo sauce is made without heavy cream or cream cheese, yet it is still completely, irresistibly creamy and loaded with tons of flavor. The one-pot cooking allows the noodles to soak up all of that garlic and Parmesan glory and still keeps dishwashing to a minimum. Need I say more?

ONE-POT GARLIC PARMESAN PASTA

SERVES 2   PREP TIME: 5 MINUTES   TOTAL TIME: 27 MINUTES   KF

1 tablespoon olive oil

4 cloves garlic, minced

2 cups reduced-sodium chicken broth

1 cup whole milk, or more as needed

2 tablespoons unsalted butter

8 ounces dried fettuccine

Kosher salt and freshly ground black pepper, to taste

¼ cup freshly grated Parmesan cheese

2 tablespoons chopped fresh parsley leaves, for garnish, optional

1. Heat the olive oil in a large stockpot or Dutch oven over medium-high heat. Add the garlic, and cook, stirring frequently, until fragrant, about 1 minute.

2. Stir in the chicken broth, milk, butter, and uncooked fettuccine; season with salt and pepper to taste.

3. Bring to a boil; reduce the heat and simmer, stirring occasionally, until the pasta is cooked through, 15 to 17 minutes. Stir in the cheese. If the mixture is too thick, add more milk as needed until desired consistency is reached.

4. Serve immediately, garnished with parsley, if desired.

PER SERVING: CALORIES 742 FAT 28.8g PROTEIN 26g CARB 93g FIBER 4g CHOL 61mg IRON 4mg SODIUM 943mg CALC 367mg

TIP
Replacing the whipping cream with milk lightens this recipe substantially. Whole milk has 80% fewer calories than whipping cream.

This may just be the easiest, most no-fuss comfort soup you will ever make. Use fresh tortellini, which can be found in the refrigerated section of your local grocery store. Pick up any kind of tortellini—spinach, mushroom, pesto—it's up to you!

ONE-POT SPINACH and TOMATO TORTELLINI SOUP

SERVES 4   PREP TIME: 8 MINUTES   TOTAL TIME: 25 MINUTES   KF

1 tablespoon olive oil

3 cloves garlic, minced

1 onion, diced

4 cups reduced-sodium chicken broth

1 (14.5-ounce) can petite diced tomatoes, undrained

1 (9-ounce) package refrigerated three-cheese tortellini

½ teaspoon dried basil

½ teaspoon dried oregano

1 bay leaf

Kosher salt and freshly ground black pepper, to taste

3 cups loosely packed baby spinach, chopped

2 tablespoons freshly grated Parmesan cheese, for garnish

1. Heat the olive oil in a large stockpot or Dutch oven over medium heat. Add the garlic and onion, and cook, stirring frequently, until the onions have become translucent, 2 to 3 minutes.

2. Whisk in the chicken broth, diced tomatoes and their juices, tortellini, basil, oregano, bay leaf, and 1 cup water; season with salt and pepper to taste.

3. Bring to a boil; reduce the heat, and simmer until the tortellini is cooked through, 5 to 6 minutes. Stir in the spinach until it begins to wilt, about 2 minutes. Remove and discard bay leaf.

4. Serve immediately, garnished with the cheese.

PER SERVING: CALORIES 308 **FAT** 8.7g **PROTEIN** 19g **CARB** 38g **FIBER** 8g **CHOL** 30mg **IRON** 3mg **SODIUM** 1152mg **CALC** 214mg

Making pasta has never been easier, or tastier, than this. This meal in a bowl requires just a few ingredients, yet it's creamy, hearty, and sure to be a hit with the entire family. This is one of my most popular recipes—it has been shared over 1 million times!

ONE-POT ZUCCHINI MUSHROOM PASTA

SERVES 4   PREP TIME: 5 MINUTES   TOTAL TIME: 30 MINUTES   KF   VEG

2 tablespoons olive oil

2 (8-ounce) packages sliced cremini mushrooms

2 zucchini, quartered and thinly sliced crosswise

3 cloves garlic, minced

²/₃ cup frozen peas, thawed

1 pound dried spaghetti

4 sprigs fresh thyme

¹/₃ cup freshly grated Parmesan cheese

¹/₂ cup heavy cream

Kosher salt and freshly ground black pepper, to taste

1. Heat 1 tablespoon of the olive oil in a large stockpot or Dutch oven over medium-high heat. Add the mushrooms, and cook for about 5 minutes, stirring occasionally, until the liquid evaporates and the mushrooms are lightly browned. Transfer the mushrooms to a bowl, and set aside.

2. Add the remaining 1 tablespoon olive oil to the pot; add the zucchini and garlic. Cook for about 4 minutes, stirring frequently so the garlic doesn't burn, until tender and beginning to brown. Transfer the zucchini and garlic to the bowl with the mushrooms, and stir in the peas.

3. Stir 4 ¹/₂ cups water, the spaghetti, and the thyme sprigs into the pot. Bring to a boil; reduce the heat to medium, and simmer, uncovered, until the pasta is cooked through and the liquid has reduced, 10 to 11 minutes. Stir in the cheese and heavy cream. Stir in the vegetables. Season generously with salt and pepper to taste, and serve immediately.

PER SERVING: CALORIES 690 FAT 23g PROTEIN 24g CARB 98g FIBER 7g CHOL 48mg IRON 5mg SODIUM 332mg CALC 203mg

TIP

Going meatless has never been tastier! Many people still consume too much meat, but easy vegetarian options can help balance your diet.

You can make restaurant-quality egg drop soup at home with ingredients that you probably already have on hand. If you like, add in more veggies like snow peas, bean sprouts, or mushrooms. This is perfect comfort on rainy days.

CHICKEN *and* CORN EGG DROP SOUP

SERVES 4   PREP TIME: 10 MINUTES   TOTAL TIME: 20 MINUTES   `KF`

1 tablespoon vegetable oil

1 pound ground chicken (see Note)

6 cups reduced-sodium chicken broth

1 tablespoon reduced-sodium soy sauce

1 tablespoon freshly grated ginger

3 large eggs, lightly beaten

2 cups corn kernels, frozen and thawed, canned, or roasted

1 green onion, thinly sliced, for garnish, optional

1 tablespoon sesame seeds, for garnish, optional

1. Heat the oil in a large stockpot or Dutch oven over medium heat. Add the ground chicken, and cook until browned, 3 to 5 minutes, making sure to crumble the chicken as it cooks. Drain any excess fat, and transfer the browned meat to a plate; set aside.

2. Combine the chicken broth, soy sauce, and ginger in the same pot over medium heat. Bring to a boil; reduce the heat, and simmer.

3. Gradually add the eggs in a slow steady stream, stirring with a fork. Cook until the eggs are set, stirring frequently to create ribbons, about 2 minutes.

4. Stir in the reserved chicken and the corn until heated through, 2 to 3 minutes.

5. Serve immediately, garnished with the green onion and sesame seeds, if desired.

Note: Ground pork can be substituted for the chicken.

PER SERVING: CALORIES 373 FAT 17.8g PROTEIN 38g CARB 16g FIBER 1g CHOL 238mg IRON 2mg SODIUM 998mg CALC 29mg

Making soup from scratch drastically cuts down on your sodium intake. Even the "low-sodium" types of canned soups are loaded with salt. You also get a lot more veggies per serving when you make it yourself. One bowl of this creamy soup gives you two servings of vegetables. Best of all, this can be made in 30 minutes, start to finish.

CREAMY CHICKEN *and* MUSHROOM SOUP

SERVES 6   **PREP TIME:** 15 MINUTES   **TOTAL TIME:** 30 MINUTES

1 tablespoon olive oil

8 ounces boneless, skinless chicken thighs, cut into 1-inch chunks

Kosher salt and freshly ground black pepper

2 tablespoons unsalted butter

3 cloves garlic, minced

8 ounces cremini mushrooms, thinly sliced

1 onion, diced

3 carrots, peeled and diced

2 stalks celery, diced

½ teaspoon dried thyme

¼ cup all-purpose flour

4 cups chicken stock

1 bay leaf

½ cup half-and-half, plus more as needed (see Note)

2 tablespoons chopped fresh parsley leaves, for garnish, optional

1 sprig fresh rosemary, for garnish, optional

1. Heat the olive oil in a large stockpot or Dutch oven over medium heat. Season chicken thighs with salt and pepper. Add the chicken to the stockpot, and cook until golden, 2 to 3 minutes; set aside.

2. Melt the butter in the stockpot or Dutch oven over medium heat. Add the garlic, mushrooms, onion, carrots, and celery. Cook, stirring occasionally, until tender, 3 to 4 minutes. Stir in the thyme until fragrant, about 1 minute.

3. Whisk in the flour until lightly browned, about 1 minute. Whisk in the chicken stock, bay leaf, and chicken thighs, and cook, whisking constantly, until slightly thickened, 4 to 5 minutes.

4. Stir in the half-and-half until heated through, 1 to 2 minutes; season with salt and pepper to taste. If the soup is too thick, add more half-and-half as needed until desired consistency is reached.

5. Serve immediately, garnished with parsley and rosemary, if desired.

Note: Half-and-half is equal parts of whole milk and cream. For 1 cup half-and-half, you can substitute ¾ cup whole milk + ¼ cup heavy cream or ⅔ cup skim or low-fat milk + ⅓ cup heavy cream.

PER SERVING: CALORIES 190 **FAT** 9.9g **PROTEIN** 12g **CARB** 15g **FIBER** 2g **CHOL** 48mg **IRON** 1mg **SODIUM** 570mg **CALC** 59mg

Yes, you can make your own mac and cheese completely from scratch right in the microwave, and it all comes together in a single bowl. This is especially great when you're cooking for one and want something better for dinner than a bowl of cereal while wearing your hot pink sweatpants. (But no judgement either way.)

MICROWAVE MAC and CHEESE FOR ONE

SERVES 1   PREP TIME: 5 MINUTES   TOTAL TIME: 15 MINUTES   KF

½ cup dried macaroni

⅓ cup whole milk, plus more as needed

¼ teaspoon salt

⅓ cup shredded Monterey Jack cheese

⅓ cup shredded Gruyère cheese

1 tablespoon freshly grated Parmesan cheese

½ teaspoon Dijon mustard

Freshly ground black pepper, to taste

1 teaspoon chopped fresh parsley leaves, for garnish, optional

1. In a medium microwave-safe bowl, combine the pasta, milk, and salt. Stir in ½ cup water.

2. Place the bowl in the microwave, and cook at high in 2-minute intervals, or until al dente, adding up to an additional ¼ cup water as needed and stirring between intervals, 6 to 8 minutes total (see Note).

3. Stir in the Jack, Gruyère, and Parmesan, along with the mustard and additional milk if needed; season with pepper to taste.

4. Return to the microwave and cook at high for 30 seconds to 1 minute more, until the cheeses have melted; stir until smooth.

5. Serve immediately, garnished with parsley, if desired.

Note: Cooking times will vary depending on the power of your microwave.

PER SERVING: CALORIES 560 **FAT** 29.2g **PROTEIN** 30g **CARB** 45g **FIBER** 2g **CHOL** 96mg **IRON** 1mg **SODIUM** 1199mg **CALC** 807mg

TIP

This is best served immediately, but if you need to reheat, add milk, one tablespoon at a time, until the desired consistency is reached.

Risotto doesn't have to be a labor-intensive process involving hours of endless stirring. This microwave version is done in minutes, and it serves just one so you don't have to share with anyone!

MUSHROOM *and* THYME RISOTTO FOR ONE

SERVES 1 **PREP TIME:** 10 MINUTES **TOTAL TIME:** 20 MINUTES `GF`

1 tablespoon unsalted butter

2 tablespoons chopped onion

1 clove garlic, minced

⅓ cup vegetable broth, plus more as needed

¼ cup Arborio rice

2 tablespoons white wine

¼ cup mushrooms, such as white, cremini, oyster, chanterelle, or shiitake

¼ cup loosely packed baby arugula or baby spinach

1 teaspoon fresh thyme leaves

Kosher salt and freshly ground black pepper, to taste

1 tablespoon freshly grated Parmesan cheese

1 sprig fresh thyme, for garnish, optional

1. In a microwave-safe 12-ounce mug or bowl, combine the butter, onion, and garlic. Cover the mug, and cook in the microwave at high for 60 seconds.

2. Stir in the vegetable broth and rice. Return to the microwave, cover, and cook in 2-minute intervals until tender, stirring and adding additional broth 1 tablespoon at a time, if necessary for desired consistency, 6 to 8 minutes total (see Note).

3. Stir in the wine, mushrooms, arugula, and thyme; season with salt and pepper to taste. Return to the microwave, covered, and cook until the mushrooms are tender, 1 to 2 minutes more.

4. Serve immediately, sprinkled with the Parmesan and garnished with a thyme sprig, if desired.

Note: Cooking times will vary depending on the power of your microwave.

PER SERVING: CALORIES 332 **FAT** 12.2g **PROTEIN** 5g **CARB** 44g **FIBER** 3g **CHOL** 31mg **IRON** 1mg **SODIUM** 801mg **CALC** 38mg

This is one of those effortless meals where everything—and I mean everything—is cooked on a single baking sheet. The veggies are first par-roasted for 7 minutes to get a nice head start, and then the steaks are added to broil to your desired doneness. Serve this straight from the sheet pan to save on dishes.

SHEET-PAN STEAK *and* VEGGIES

SERVES 4   PREP TIME: 10 MINUTES   TOTAL TIME: 25 MINUTES   `GF` `KF`

FOR THE FRESH HERB BUTTER

4 tablespoons unsalted butter, at room temperature

1 tablespoon chopped fresh basil

1 tablespoon chopped fresh thyme

1 tablespoon chopped fresh rosemary

Kosher salt and freshly ground black pepper, to taste

1 pound asparagus, trimmed

1 pound baby carrots, peeled, trimmed, and cut in half lengthwise

2 cups cherry tomatoes

2 tablespoons olive oil

3 cloves garlic, minced

1 teaspoon dried thyme

Kosher salt and freshly ground black pepper, to taste

2 pounds top sirloin steak, 1 inch thick, patted dry (see Note)

1. Preheat the oven to broil. Lightly oil a baking sheet, or coat it with nonstick spray.

2. Make the fresh herb butter: Mix together the butter, basil, thyme, and rosemary in a small bowl until the herbs are evenly incorporated; season with salt and pepper to taste. Set aside.

3. Spread out the asparagus, carrots, and tomatoes in a single layer on the prepared baking sheet. Add the olive oil, garlic, and thyme; season with salt and pepper to taste. Gently toss to combine.

4. Broil the mixed veggies 6 inches from the heat source for about 7 minutes, until the carrots are slightly tender.

5. Remove the baking sheet from the oven. Season the steaks with salt and pepper to taste, and add them to the baking sheet in a single layer.

6. Return to the oven, and broil until browned and charred at the edges, about 2 minutes per side for medium-rare, or until desired doneness.

7. Serve immediately with the fresh herb butter.

Note: You can also use hangar, flank, or New York strip steak.

PER SERVING: CALORIES 567 **FAT** 30.2g **PROTEIN** 60g **CARB** 17g **FIBER** 6g **CHOL** 180mg **IRON** 8mg **SODIUM** 482mg **CALC** 95mg

Completely baked from start to finsh.

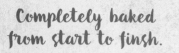

The quickest beef and broccoli ever.

3

(BETTER THAN) TAKEOUT EXPRESS

No more waiting for the delivery guy. In just 20 to 30 minutes you can make your own copycats of favorite restaurant dishes at a fraction of restaurant prices. Plus, the homemade versions always taste a million times better.

All the flavors of a traditional BBQ chicken pizza without any of the fuss. There's absolutely no kneading, no rolling, no tricky anything involved here. Simply add everything on top of a crusty French bread loaf and you are done!

BBQ CHICKEN FRENCH BREAD PIZZA

SERVES 8   PREP TIME: 10 MINUTES   TOTAL TIME: 24 MINUTES   KF

1 tablespoon olive oil

1 pound boneless, skinless chicken breasts, diced

1/4 teaspoon kosher salt

1/8 teaspoon freshly ground black pepper

3/4 cup barbecue sauce, divided

1 (1-pound) French bread loaf, cut in half horizontally

1 cup thinly sliced red onion

1 cup shredded Cheddar cheese

1 cup shredded mozzarella cheese

2 tablespoons chopped fresh cilantro leaves, for garnish, optional

1. Preheat the oven to 400°F. Line a baking sheet with parchment paper.

2. Heat the oil in a large skillet or Dutch oven over medium-high heat.

3. Season the chicken with salt and pepper. Add the chicken to the skillet, and cook, stirring occasionally, until lightly browned and cooked through, 3 to 4 minutes. Stir in 1/4 cup barbecue sauce, and set aside.

4. Place the bread, cut-sides up, onto the prepared baking sheet. Spread the remaining barbecue sauce evenly over the bread slices; top with the chicken, red onion, and cheeses.

5. Bake for 10 minutes, or until the cheese has melted.

6. Serve immediately, garnished with additional barbecue sauce and cilantro, if desired.

PER SERVING: CALORIES 382 FAT 11.8g PROTEIN 26g CARB 42g FIBER 2g CHOL 55mg IRON 3mg SODIUM 889mg CALC 238mg

TIP

When you make pizza at home, you can control the salt levels and load up on healthier ingredients like veggies and chicken!

These egg rolls are inspired by the ones from The Cheesecake Factory. I dedicate them to all you avocado lovers out there. And if you're not a keen avocado fan, these will still blow your mind. Seriously.

AVOCADO EGG ROLLS

MAKES 8 EGG ROLLS   PREP TIME: 15 MINUTES   TOTAL TIME: 20 MINUTES   KF VEG

FOR THE CILANTRO DIPPING SAUCE

¾ cup loosely packed fresh cilantro leaves

⅓ cup sour cream

2 tablespoons mayonnaise

1 jalapeño chile, seeded and deveined, optional

1 clove garlic

Juice of 1 lime

Kosher salt and freshly ground black pepper, to taste

3 ripe avocados, pitted and peeled

1 Roma tomato, diced

¼ cup diced red onion

2 tablespoons chopped fresh cilantro leaves

Juice of 1 lime

Kosher salt and freshly ground black pepper, to taste

1 cup vegetable oil

8 egg roll wrappers

1. Make the cilantro dipping sauce: Combine the cilantro, sour cream, mayonnaise, jalapeño, garlic, and lime juice in the bowl of a food processor, and pulse until all the ingredients are evenly incorporated; season with salt and pepper to taste. Set aside.

2. In a medium bowl, gently mash the avocados using a potato masher. Add the tomato, red onion, cilantro, and lime juice, and gently stir to combine. Season with salt and pepper to taste.

3. Heat the oil in a large skillet or Dutch oven over medium-high heat, until it registers 350°F using a deep-fry thermometer.

4. Working with one wrapper at a time, place about ¼ cup avocado mixture in the center of the wrapper. Bring the bottom edge of the wrapper tightly over the filling, and then fold in the sides. Continue to roll up the wrapper, enclosing the filling, until the top of the wrapper is reached. Using your finger, rub the top edge of the wrapper with a dab of water, pressing to seal. Repeat with the remaining wrappers and avocado mixture.

5. Working in batches, add the egg rolls to the hot oil, and fry until golden brown and crispy, 2 to 3 minutes per side. Using tongs, transfer the egg rolls to a paper towel–lined plate to drain.

6. Serve immediately with the cilantro dipping sauce.

PER SERVING: CALORIES 317 FAT 22.5g PROTEIN 4g CARB 26g FIBER 5g CHOL 11mg IRON 2mg SODIUM 330mg CALC 27mg

This recipe gives you egg rolls that are restaurant quality without that heavy grease, and you can throw in any veggies you happen to have on hand. Mushrooms, broccoli, snap peas, and bean sprouts would all make great additions. To keep these meatless, just switch out the the ground chicken for crumbled tofu.

COPYCAT TAKEOUT EGG ROLLS

MAKES 8 EGG ROLLS   PREP TIME: 20 MINUTES   TOTAL TIME: 30 MINUTES   KF

1 pound cooked ground chicken

2 cups shredded cabbage

1 carrot, grated

1 stalk celery, diced

2 cloves garlic, minced

2 green onions, thinly sliced

1 tablespoon reduced-sodium soy sauce

1 tablespoon sesame oil

1 tablespoon hoisin sauce

1 tablespoon freshly grated ginger

1 teaspoon Sriracha sauce, optional

1 cup vegetable oil

8 egg roll wrappers

1. In a medium bowl, combine the chicken, cabbage, carrot, celery, garlic, green onions, soy sauce, sesame oil, hoisin, ginger, and Sriracha, if desired, and stir to evenly distribute the ingredients.

2. Heat the oil in a large skillet or Dutch oven over medium-high heat, until it registers 350°F using a deep-fry thermometer.

3. Working with one wrapper at a time, place about ¼ cup chicken mixture in the center of the wrapper. Bring the bottom edge of the wrapper tightly over the filling, and then fold in the sides. Continue to roll up the wrapper, enclosing the filling, until the top of the wrapper is reached. Using your finger, rub the top edge of the wrapper with a dab of water, pressing to seal. Repeat with the remaining wrappers and chicken mixture.

4. Working in batches, add the egg rolls to the hot oil, and fry until evenly golden brown and crispy, 2 to 3 minutes. Transfer to a paper towel–lined plate to drain.

5. Serve immediately.

PER SERVING: CALORIES 300 **FAT** 17.1g **PROTEIN** 15g **CARB** 22g **FIBER** 1g **CHOL** 56mg **IRON** 2mg **SODIUM** 334mg **CALC** 67mg

TIP

Serve these with a dipping sauce such as plum sauce or sweet and sour.

When I had my first job as a 16-year-old working at Cold Stone Creamery, I remember ordering the kid's meal at Panda Express next door. This wasn't because I didn't eat much, but more to save a few bucks. If only I knew I could make their chow mein for less than half the price, I would've had a full-sized portion for breakfast, lunch, and dinner.

EXPRESS CHOW MEIN

SERVES 4   PREP TIME: 10 MINUTES   TOTAL TIME: 20 MINUTES   KF

½ cup reduced-sodium soy sauce

6 cloves garlic, minced

2 tablespoons packed brown sugar

4 teaspoons freshly grated ginger

½ teaspoon ground white pepper

2 (5.6-ounce) packages refrigerated yakisoba noodles, seasoning sauce packets discarded (see Note)

2 tablespoons olive oil

1 onion, diced

3 stalks celery, sliced on a diagonal

2 cups shredded cabbage

1. In a small bowl, whisk together the soy sauce, garlic, brown sugar, ginger, and white pepper; set aside.

2. In a large pot of boiling water, cook the yakisoba noodles (they'll start off in a clump) until loosened, 1 to 2 minutes; drain well.

3. Heat the olive oil in a large skillet over medium-high heat. Add the onion and celery, and cook, stirring often, until tender, about 4 minutes. Stir in the cabbage until heated through, about 1 minute.

4. Add the noodles and the soy sauce mixture, and toss until the ingredients are evenly distributed, about 2 minutes. Serve immediately.

Note: Yakisoba noodles can be found in the refrigerated aisle of most grocery stores.

PER SERVING: CALORIES 265 FAT 8.3g PROTEIN 9g CARB 48g FIBER 4g CHOL 2mg IRON 1mg SODIUM 1254mg CALC 53mg

The only "faux" part of this cheater pad thai recipe is the use of Italian-style linguine noodles instead of traditional rice noodles. The latter can be difficult to find and will result in gluey, clumpy noodles if overcooked or prepared incorrectly. Use linguine and you'll get to enjoy all of the wonderful pad thai flavors without dealing with anything tricky.

FAUX SHRIMP PAD THAI

SERVES 4   PREP TIME: 10 MINUTES   TOTAL TIME: 20 MINUTES

FOR THE SAUCE

3 tablespoons reduced-sodium soy sauce

2 tablespoons packed brown sugar

1 tablespoon fish sauce

1 teaspoon sambal oelek (ground fresh chile paste), plus more to taste

Juice of 1 lime

8 ounces dried linguine

1 cup bean sprouts

1 tablespoon vegetable oil

2 cloves garlic, minced

8 ounces medium shrimp, peeled and deveined

¼ teaspoon freshly ground black pepper

2 large eggs, lightly beaten

1 carrot, grated

2 green onions, thinly sliced

¼ cup peanuts, chopped

¼ cup fresh cilantro leaves

1 lime, cut into wedges, for garnish

1. Make the sauce: In a small bowl, whisk together the soy sauce, brown sugar, fish sauce, sambal oelek, lime juice, and 1 tablespoon water; set aside.

2. In a large pot of boiling salted water, cook the pasta according to package instructions. Just 2 minutes before the pasta is cooked, add the bean sprouts; drain well.

3. Meanwhile, heat the oil in a large skillet over medium-high heat. Add garlic, and cook, stirring frequently, until fragrant, about 1 minute. Add the shrimp and black pepper, and cook, stirring occasionally, until the shrimp are pink, 2 to 3 minutes.

4. Add the pasta and sauce to the skillet, and gently toss to combine. Make a well in the center of the skillet, and pour in the beaten eggs. Stir in the eggs until cooked through and well combined, about 2 minutes (see Note).

5. Serve immediately, topped with the carrot, green onions, peanuts, and cilantro, and garnished with the lime wedges, if desired.

Note: If you want bigger chunks of eggs, scramble them separately, chop, and toss them back into the skillet near the end of cooking.

PER SERVING: CALORIES 435 FAT 11.8g PROTEIN 25g CARB 58g FIBER 4g CHOL 173mg IRON 3mg SODIUM 904mg CALC 78mg

This easy stir-fry uses ingredients you may already have on hand. Just use standard spaghetti noodles, fettuccine, or even angel hair pasta and skip the last-minute grocery run. You're welcome.

ASIAN GARLIC NOODLES

SERVES 4   PREP TIME: 10 MINUTES   TOTAL TIME: 20 MINUTES

FOR THE GARLIC SAUCE

⅓ cup reduced-sodium soy sauce

2 tablespoons packed brown sugar

1 tablespoon sambal oelek (ground fresh chile paste; see Note), plus more to taste

1 tablespoon oyster sauce

1 tablespoon freshly grated ginger

1 teaspoon sesame oil

3 cloves garlic, minced

8 ounces dried spaghetti

1 tablespoon olive oil

12 ounces medium shrimp, peeled and deveined

8 ounces cremini mushrooms, sliced

1 red bell pepper, diced

2 zucchini, trimmed and diced

1 carrot, grated

2 tablespoons chopped fresh cilantro leaves, for garnish, optional

1. Make the garlic sauce: In a small bowl, whisk together the soy sauce, brown sugar, sambal oelek, oyster sauce, ginger, sesame oil, and garlic. Set aside.

2. In a large pot of boiling salted water, cook the pasta according to package instructions; drain well.

3. Meanwhile, heat the olive oil in a large skillet over medium-high heat. Add the shrimp and 2 tablespoons of the garlic sauce, and cook, stirring occasionally, until the shrimp are pink, 2 to 3 minutes. Set aside.

4. Stir the mushrooms, bell pepper, zucchini, and carrot into the skillet. Cook, stirring frequently, until vegetables are tender, 3 to 4 minutes. Add the spaghetti, shrimp, and remaining garlic sauce mixture to the pan, and toss until the ingredients are heated through and evenly distributed, 2 to 3 minutes.

5. Serve immediately, garnished with the cilantro, if desired.

Note: Sriracha sauce can be substituted for the sambal oelek, if desired.

PER SERVING: CALORIES 414 FAT 6g PROTEIN 27g CARB 62g FIBER 4g CHOL 119mg IRON 3mg SODIUM 1053mg CALC 92mg

Kimchi fried rice is one of my go-to comfort dishes. I like my fried rice lighter and healthier than your standard takeout version, so this recipe uses brown rice—instead of the typical white rice—and tons of veggies. You can skip the beaten egg, if you like, and top with a fried egg with an oozing yolk instead!

KIMCHI FRIED RICE

SERVES 6 PREP TIME: 10 MINUTES TOTAL TIME: 25 MINUTES `VEG`

¼ cup kimchi juice

1 tablespoon reduced-sodium soy sauce

1 tablespoon freshly grated ginger

1 teaspoon sesame oil

1 tablespoon gochujang (hot pepper paste), optional

2 tablespoons olive oil

2 large eggs, lightly beaten

2 cloves garlic, minced

1 onion, diced

1 cup chopped kimchi (see Note)

2 carrots, peeled and diced

½ cup frozen, canned, or roasted corn kernels

½ cup frozen or canned peas

3 cups cooked leftover brown rice (see Note)

2 green onions, sliced

1 teaspoon sesame seeds, for garnish, optional

1. In a small bowl, whisk together the kimchi juice, soy sauce, ginger, sesame oil, and gochujang, if desired. Set aside.

2. Heat 1 tablespoon of the olive oil in a medium skillet over low heat. Pour in the beaten eggs to cover the bottom of the pan, and let them cook like an omelet, 2 to 3 minutes per side, flipping only once. Let cool before dicing the eggs into small pieces.

3. Heat the remaining 1 tablespoon olive oil in a large skillet or wok over medium-high heat. Add the garlic, onion, and kimchi to the skillet, and cook, stirring often, until the onions have become translucent and the kimchi is starting to brown, 3 to 4 minutes.

4. Stir in the carrots, corn, and peas, and cook, stirring constantly, until the vegetables are tender, 3 to 4 minutes.

5. Stir in the rice, green onions, eggs, and kimchi juice mixture. Cook, stirring constantly, until heated through, about 2 minutes. Serve immediately, garnished with the sesame seeds, if desired.

Note: Kimchi is now available in the produce aisle of many grocery stores. For best results, use cold leftover rice.

PER SERVING: CALORIES 233 FAT 8g PROTEIN 7g CARB 34g FIBER 4g CHOL 62mg IRON 1mg SODIUM 428mg CALC 46mg

This copycat recipe from PF Chang's is not only budget friendly, it comes together super fast. It's versatile, too: Swap out the ground chicken for ground turkey, beef, or even cubes of tofu. And go ahead, toss in more veggies like carrots, zucchini, or mushrooms. I'm not going to lie—this is my favorite recipe. Period.

CHICKEN LETTUCE WRAPS

SERVES 4   PREP TIME: 10 MINUTES   TOTAL TIME: 20 MINUTES   KF

1 tablespoon olive oil

1 pound ground chicken (see Note)

2 cloves garlic, minced

1 onion, diced

¼ cup plus 1 tablespoon hoisin sauce

2 tablespoons reduced-sodium soy sauce

1 tablespoon rice wine vinegar

1 tablespoon freshly grated ginger

1 teaspoon Sriracha sauce, plus more to taste

1 (8-ounce) can whole water chestnuts, drained and diced

2 green onions, thinly sliced

Freshly ground black pepper, to taste

2 heads butter lettuce, cores removed to separate the leaves

1. Heat the olive oil in a large skillet over medium-high heat. Add the ground chicken, and cook until browned, about 6 minutes, making sure to crumble the chicken as it cooks; drain off excess fat, if any.

2. Stir the garlic, onion, hoisin sauce, soy sauce, vinegar, ginger, and Sriracha into the chicken; cook over medium-high heat until the onions have become translucent, 1 to 2 minutes. Stir in the water chestnuts and green onions, and cook until tender, 1 to 2 minutes; season with pepper to taste.

3. To serve, spoon several tablespoons of the chicken mixture into the center of each lettuce leaf, taco style.

Note: Try a mix of light and dark chicken meat.

PER SERVING: CALORIES 271 FAT 11.9g PROTEIN 23g CARB 20g FIBER 4g CHOL 92mg IRON 2mg SODIUM 691mg CALC 61mg

Another restaurant favorite that can easily be made in your own kitchen, this is one of my most popular recipes. It makes the most amazingly crisp chicken bites and a sweet chili mayo sauce that's so good, you may be tempted to eat it with a spoon.

BANG-BANG CHICKEN

SERVES 4   PREP TIME: 15 MINUTES   TOTAL TIME: 30 MINUTES   `KF`

FOR THE SWEET CHILI MAYO SAUCE

1/4 cup mayonnaise

2 tablespoons sweet chili sauce

1 tablespoon honey

2 teaspoons hot sauce (such as Frank's RedHot Sauce)

1 cup vegetable oil, plus more as needed

1 cup buttermilk

3/4 cup all-purpose flour

1/2 cup cornstarch

1 large egg

1 tablespoon hot sauce

1/2 teaspoon kosher salt

1/4 teaspoon freshly ground black pepper

2 boneless, skinless chicken breasts (about 1 1/4 pounds), cut into 1-inch chunks

2 cups panko (see Note)

1. Make the sweet chili mayo sauce: Whisk together the mayonnaise, sweet chili sauce, honey, and hot sauce in a small bowl; set aside.

2. Heat the oil in a large skillet over medium-high heat.

3. In a large bowl, whisk together the buttermilk, flour, cornstarch, egg, hot sauce, salt, and pepper. Add the chicken pieces, and toss to coat.

4. Working with one piece at a time, dredge the chicken in the panko, pressing to make sure each piece is evenly coated. Set aside.

5. Working in batches, fry the chicken in the skillet until evenly golden and crispy on all sides, 2 to 3 minutes total. Transfer to a paper towel–lined plate to drain.

6. Serve immediately, drizzled with the sweet chili mayo sauce.

Note: Panko is a Japanese-style of bread crumbs that can be found in the Asian section of your local grocery store.

PER SERVING: CALORIES 636 FAT 27.9g PROTEIN 38.5g CARB 59g FIBER 2g CHOL 134mg IRON 2mg SODIUM 601mg CALC 22mg

It doesn't get much easier than this. Drop your drumsticks into the marinade before leaving for work (I promise, it'll only take 5 minutes!). When you get home, coat the chicken in the cornflakes and pop it into the oven. These drumsticks are so crisp, no one will ever guess they're baked from start to finish.

BUTTERMILK RANCH DRUMSTICKS

SERVES 4 **PREP TIME:** 10 MINUTES **TOTAL TIME:** 55 MINUTES PLUS MARINATING **KF**

1 cup buttermilk

2 teaspoons dried parsley

2 teaspoons garlic powder

2 teaspoons onion powder

2 teaspoons dried dill

2 teaspoons dried mustard

1 teaspoon kosher salt

½ teaspoon freshly ground black pepper

8 skinless chicken drumsticks

½ cup all-purpose flour

2 large eggs, beaten

6 cups cornflakes, coarsely crushed (see Note)

Vegetable oil or nonstick cooking spray

1 tablespoon chopped fresh parsley leaves, for garnish, optional

1. To a gallon-sized zip-top bag or large bowl, add the buttermilk, parsley, garlic powder, onion powder, dill, mustard, salt, and pepper. Shake or stir to combine, and then add the drumsticks. Marinate for a minimum of 6 hours or overnight, turning the bag or rotating the drumsticks occasionally. Drain the chicken.

2. Preheat the oven to 400°F. Place an oven-safe rack on a baking sheet, and lightly oil the rack or coat it with nonstick spray.

3. Working in batches, dredge the chicken in the flour, eggs, and then the crushed cornflakes, pressing to make sure each drumstick is evenly coated with the crumbs. Arrange on the prepared rack in a single layer, and coat each piece with vegetable oil.

4. Bake until the drumsticks are golden brown and completely cooked through, 40 to 45 minutes. (A meat thermometer inserted into the thickest part of a drumstick should reach an internal temperature of 165°F.)

5. Serve immediately, garnished with parsley, if desired.

Note: Crush the cornflakes by putting them in a zip-top bag and then pressing down with the heel of your hand or the bottom of a cup.

PER SERVING: CALORIES 554 FAT 13.2g PROTEIN 56.5g CARB 50g FIBER 2g CHOL 312mg IRON 16mg SODIUM 759mg CALC 76mg

The most time-consuming part of this recipe is waiting for the rice to cook. But if you have leftover rice from the night before, these bowls will come together in just 10 minutes! For added protein, the rice can easily be swapped out for quinoa. After you try this, you won't need to step into Chipotle again.

EASY BURRITO BOWLS

SERVES 6   **PREP TIME:** 10 MINUTES   **TOTAL TIME:** 25 MINUTES   `GF` `KF` `VEG`

FOR THE CHIPOTLE CREAM SAUCE

1 cup sour cream

1 tablespoon chipotle paste (see Note)

1 clove garlic, crushed in a garlic press

Juice of 1 lime

1/4 teaspoon salt, plus more to taste

1 cup uncooked white rice

1 cup salsa

3 cups chopped romaine lettuce (about 8 ounces)

1 (15 1/4-ounce) can whole-kernel corn, drained

1 (15-ounce) can black beans, drained and rinsed

2 Roma tomatoes, diced

1 ripe avocado, pitted, peeled, and diced

2 tablespoons chopped fresh cilantro leaves

1. Make the chipotle cream sauce: In a small bowl, whisk together the sour cream, chipotle paste, garlic, lime juice, and salt; set aside.

2. In a large saucepan, combine the rice and 1 1/2 cups of water, and cook according to package instructions; let cool, and then stir in the salsa; set aside.

3. Assemble the bowls: Divide the rice mixture among serving bowls; top each evenly with the lettuce, corn, black beans, tomatoes, avocado, and cilantro.

4. Serve immediately, drizzled with the chipotle cream sauce.

Note: Chipotle paste can be found in most large supermarkets or anywhere Mexican foods are sold. Or substitute 2 tablespoons chipotle peppers in adobo sauce.

PER SERVING: CALORIES 360 **FAT** 12.1g **PROTEIN** 10g **CARB** 53g **FIBER** 10g **CHOL** 28mg **IRON** 2mg **SODIUM** 743mg **CALC** 98mg

Here's a fun take on everyone's favorite beef and broccoli takeout dish, except you can use the ground beef you've been storing in your freezer. This cooks up quickly, and you can swap out the ground beef for ground turkey or chicken, or switch the rice for quinoa. Whichever variations you choose, dinner will be on the table before you can even find your stash of takeout menus.

BEEF *and* BROCCOLI BOWLS

SERVES 4   PREP TIME: 10 MINUTES   TOTAL TIME: 20 MINUTES   KF

½ cup reduced-sodium soy sauce

2 tablespoons packed brown sugar

2 cloves garlic, minced

1 tablespoon rice wine vinegar

1 tablespoon sesame oil

1 tablespoon freshly grated ginger

1 tablespoon Sriracha sauce, optional

1 tablespoon vegetable oil

1 pound ground beef

12 ounces broccoli florets
   (2 to 3 cups)

2 green onions, thinly sliced

2 cups leftover white or brown rice

1 teaspoon sesame seeds, for
   garnish, optional

1. In a small bowl, whisk together the soy sauce, brown sugar, garlic, vinegar, sesame oil, ginger, and Sriracha, if desired. Set aside.

2. Heat the vegetable oil in a large skillet over medium-high heat. Add the ground beef, and cook until browned, 3 to 5 minutes, making sure to crumble the beef as it cooks; drain off excess fat.

3. Stir in the broccoli, green onions, and soy sauce mixture until evenly incorporated; cover the skillet, and allow to simmer until the beef is cooked through and the broccoli is tender, 3 to 4 minutes. Stir in the rice until warmed.

4. Divide the beef and broccoli mixture among bowls, and serve immediately, garnished with the sesame seeds, if desired.

PER SERVING: CALORIES 415 FAT 14g PROTEIN 31g CARB 39g FIBER 3g CHOL 76mg IRON 4mg SODIUM 1204mg CALC 64mg

Cheesy grits and Cajun shrimp are as classic as burgers and fries. It's a match made in heaven—in 30 minutes. And it's simple enough for a weeknight meal but fancy enough to impress dinner guests. Try throwing in Andouille sausage for extra flavor.

CAJUN SHRIMP *and* GRITS

SERVES 4   PREP TIME: 15 MINUTES   TOTAL TIME: 30 MINUTES

3 cups chicken broth

1 cup uncooked quick-cooking grits

½ cup shredded Cheddar cheese

¼ cup freshly grated Parmesan cheese

2 tablespoons unsalted butter

Kosher salt and freshly ground black pepper, to taste

1 pound medium shrimp, peeled and deveined

2 teaspoons Cajun seasoning

Kosher salt and freshly ground black pepper, to taste

4 slices bacon, diced

2 tablespoons chopped fresh chives, for garnish, optional

1. Bring the chicken broth to a boil in a medium saucepan over medium-high heat; stir in the grits. Cook, stirring occasionally, until thickened, about 5 minutes. Stir in both cheeses and the butter.

2. Remove the pan from the heat; season the grits with salt and pepper to taste. Set aside but keep warm.

3. Season the shrimp with the Cajun seasoning and salt and pepper to taste; set aside.

4. Heat a large skillet over medium-high heat. Add the bacon, and cook until brown and crispy, 6 to 8 minutes. Set the bacon aside on a plate, reserving 1 tablespoon of the excess fat in the skillet.

5. Add the seasoned shrimp to the skillet, and cook, stirring occasionally, until pink, 2 to 3 minutes. Remove from the heat.

6. Divide the grits among serving bowls. Serve immediately, topped with the shrimp and bacon, and garnished with the chives, if desired.

PER SERVING: CALORIES 421 FAT 19.5g PROTEIN 32g CARB 31g FIBER 2g CHOL 209mg IRON 2mg SODIUM 1567mg CALC 238mg

It's all about this cream sauce.

This is actually cauliflower!

4

SPEEDY, SIMPLE & SKINNY

Quick, healthy, and delicious. What more can you ask for?
Being busy doesn't have to mean junk food binges when you have
these easy, satisfying recipes in your weekday rotation.

BBQ chicken salad is one of my favorite salads to order while eating out, but it can get expensive. I like to think my spin on this salad can stand up to any restaurant dish, except you can make this much cheaper at home. I whip this up as my go-to lunch at least once a week, with extra tortilla strips on my cheat days.

BBQ CHICKEN SALAD

SERVES 4   PREP TIME: 10 MINUTES   TOTAL TIME: 20 MINUTES

1 tablespoon olive oil

2 boneless, skinless chicken breasts, about ¾ inch thick

Kosher salt and freshly ground black pepper, to taste

6 cups chopped romaine lettuce (about 1 pound)

1 Roma tomato, diced

¾ cup canned drained corn kernels

¾ cup canned drained and rinsed black beans

¼ cup diced red onion

¼ cup shredded Monterey Jack cheese

½ cup shredded Cheddar cheese

¼ cup Ranch dressing

¼ cup barbecue sauce

¼ cup tortilla strips, for garnish, optional

1. Heat the olive oil in a medium skillet over medium-high heat.

2. Season the chicken breasts with salt and pepper to taste. Add to the skillet and cook, flipping once, until cooked through, 4 to 5 minutes per side. Let cool before cutting into bite-sized pieces.

3. To assemble the salad, put the lettuce in a large bowl; top with the chicken, tomato, corn, beans, red onion, and both cheeses. Pour the Ranch dressing and barbecue sauce on the salad, and gently toss to combine.

4. Serve immediately, garnished with the tortilla strips, if desired.

PER SERVING: CALORIES 390 FAT 18.3g PROTEIN 30g CARB 28g FIBER 6g CHOL 89mg IRON 2mg SODIUM 842mg CALC 198mg

This salad pairs crisp bacon with juicy apples, pears, and sweet cranberries so you get to enjoy great fall flavors all year long. And the oh-so-dreamy poppy seed dressing is made a little bit lighter with Greek yogurt instead of mayonnaise. I promise you won't be able to tell the difference!

HARVEST COBB SALAD
with POPPY SEED DRESSING

SERVES 4   PREP TIME: 15 MINUTES   TOTAL TIME: 20 MINUTES   `GF`

FOR THE POPPY SEED DRESSING

¼ cup plain Greek yogurt

¼ cup whole milk

1 tablespoon mayonnaise

1 tablespoon sugar

1 tablespoon apple cider vinegar

1 tablespoon poppy seeds

4 slices bacon, diced

5 cups chopped romaine lettuce (about 1 large head)

1½ cups cooked chicken, shredded or diced

1½ cups unpeeled diced apple,

1 cup unpeeled diced Bartlett pear

½ cup raw pecans

⅓ cup dried cranberries

⅓ cup crumbled goat cheese

1. Make the poppy seed dressing: In a small bowl, whisk together the yogurt, milk, mayonnaise, sugar, apple cider vinegar, and poppy seeds; set aside.

2. Heat a large skillet over medium-high heat. Add the diced bacon and cook until brown and crispy, 6 to 8 minutes. Transfer to a paper towel–lined plate; set aside.

3. To assemble the salad, put the lettuce in a large bowl. Arrange individual rows of bacon, chicken, apple, pear, pecans, cranberries, and goat cheese on top.

4. Serve immediately with the poppy seed dressing on the side.

PER SERVING: CALORIES 403 FAT 23.8g PROTEIN 19g CARB 32g FIBER 6g CHOL 58mg IRON 2mg SODIUM 143mg CALC 129mg

Nothing beats homemade salad dressing, especially when all it takes is 5 minutes in the food processor. Simply pulse and you're set. You can easily adjust the consistency of the dressing by adding more or less olive oil. Whether you like your dressing a little thinner or thicker, you just can't go wrong with this Tex-Mex–inspired salad.

SOUTHWESTERN CHOPPED SALAD
with CILANTRO LIME DRESSING

SERVES 4   PREP TIME: 20 MINUTES   TOTAL TIME: 30 MINUTES

FOR CILANTRO LIME DRESSING

1 cup loosely packed fresh cilantro leaves

½ cup plain Greek yogurt

2 cloves garlic

Juice of 1 lime

Pinch of salt

¼ cup olive oil

2 tablespoons apple cider vinegar

1 ¼ pounds medium shrimp, peeled and deveined

1 tablespoon Cajun seasoning

2 tablespoons olive oil

12 cups chopped romaine lettuce (about 2 pounds)

2 cups cherry tomatoes, halved

1 cup canned drained corn kernels

1 cup canned drained and rinsed black beans

¼ cup chopped fresh cilantro leaves

2 ripe avocados, pitted, peeled, and diced

½ cup tortilla strips, for garnish, optional

1. Make the cilantro lime dressing: Pulse the cilantro, yogurt, garlic, lime juice, and salt in the bowl of a food processor. With the motor running, add the olive oil and vinegar in a slow stream until emulsified; set aside.

2. In a medium bowl, toss the shrimp with the Cajun seasoning and 1 tablespoon of the olive oil. Heat the remaining 1 tablespoon olive oil in a large nonstick skillet over medium-high heat; add the shrimp, and cook, stirring occasionally, until browned and cooked through, about 5 minutes. Set the pan aside to cool slightly.

3. Assemble the salad: Put the lettuce in a large bowl; top with the tomatoes, corn, black beans, and cilantro. Pour the dressing on top of the salad, and gently toss to combine. Gently stir in the avocado.

4. Serve immediately, topped with the shrimp and garnished with the tortillas strips, if desired.

PER SERVING: CALORIES 467 **FAT** 33.6g **PROTEIN** 11g **CARB** 35g **FIBER** 14g **CHOL** 14mg **IRON** 5mg **SODIUM** 745mg **CALC** 160mg

This is my go-to salad for potlucks and dinner parties. It holds up really well, and the colors are just so vibrant. Plus, the sesame seed garnish makes it look fancy without any work! You can even add leftovers such as chicken from the night before to make this a rounded meal.

SESAME KALE SALAD

SERVES 4   PREP TIME: 15 MINUTES   TOTAL TIME: 15 MINUTES   VEG

FOR THE VINAIGRETTE

¼ cup freshly squeezed lemon juice

2 tablespoons olive oil

2 cloves garlic, pressed

1 tablespoon reduced-sodium soy sauce

1 tablespoon sesame oil

1 tablespoon brown sugar

1 teaspoon freshly grated ginger

1 bunch kale, ribs removed and leaves thinly sliced

1 bell pepper, cut into thin strips

1 ripe avocado, halved, seeded, peeled, and diced

1 carrot, peeled and shredded

¼ cup chopped almonds

2 green onions, thinly sliced

6 ounces fresh shelled edamame (about 1 cup)

1 tablespoon sesame seeds, for garnish, optional

1. Make the vinaigrette: In a small bowl, whisk together the lemon juice, olive oil, garlic, soy sauce, sesame oil, brown sugar, and ginger; set aside.

2. Assemble the salad: Put the kale in a large bowl. Top with bell pepper, avocado, carrot, almonds, green onions, and edamame. Pour the dressing on top, and gently toss to combine.

3. Serve immediately, garnished with sesame seeds, if desired.

PER SERVING: CALORIES 282 FAT 20.8g PROTEIN 8g CARB 19g FIBER 8g CHOL 0mg IRON 2mg SODIUM 333mg CALC 207mg

Avocados. I love them. I've been known to eat one by itself with just a little sprinkle of sea salt. And now, I can eat them in this creamy pasta. This dish doesn't use cream or butter—just simple, fresh ingredients. That's it. The cherry tomatoes and corn kernels add a pop of color and are another way to sneak more veggies into your diet.

AVOCADO PASTA

SERVES 4   **PREP TIME:** 10 MINUTES   **TOTAL TIME:** 20 MINUTES   `VEG`

12 ounces dried spaghetti

2 ripe avocados, halved, seeded and peeled

½ cup fresh basil leaves

2 cloves garlic

2 tablespoons freshly squeezed lemon juice

Kosher salt and freshly ground black pepper, to taste

⅓ cup olive oil

1 cup cherry tomatoes, halved

½ cup canned drained and rinsed corn kernels

1. In a large pot of boiling salted water, cook the pasta according to package instructions; drain well.

2. Make the avocado sauce: Puree the avocados, basil, garlic, and lemon juice in the bowl of a food processor; season with salt and pepper to taste. With the motor running, add the olive oil in a slow stream until emulsified; set aside.

3. In a large bowl, combine pasta, avocado sauce, cherry tomatoes, and corn.

4. Serve immediately.

PER SERVING: CALORIES 626 **FAT** 31.1g **PROTEIN** 12g **CARB** 76g **FIBER** 9g **CHOL** 0mg **IRON** 4mg **SODIUM** 214mg **CALC** 17mg

TIP
Using avocados instead of cream is a great way to exchange saturated fats for mono-unsaturated fats, which can have a positive effect on cholesterol.

Here, traditional lo mein gets a complete healthy makeover with "zoodles"—ribbons of fresh zucchini instead of pasta, no boiling required! You can stir the zucchini noodles right into the sauce, cutting down the cook time to less than 15 minutes. It's healthier and quicker. What more can you ask for?

ZUCCHINI LO MEIN

SERVES 4   PREP TIME: 10 MINUTES   TOTAL TIME: 25 MINUTES   VEG

FOR THE SAUCE

¼ cup reduced-sodium soy sauce, or more to taste

3 cloves garlic, minced

1 tablespoon freshly grated ginger

1 tablespoon light brown sugar

1 teaspoon sesame oil

1 teaspoon Sriracha sauce, plus more to taste

2 medium zucchini (about 10 ounces each), trimmed

1 tablespoon olive oil

1 red bell pepper, cut into matchstick strips

1 cup sugar snap peas, strings removed

½ cup shredded carrots

1 teaspoon sesame seeds, for garnish, optional

1. Make the sauce: In a small bowl, whisk together the soy sauce, garlic, ginger, brown sugar, sesame oil, and Sriracha; set aside.

2. Using a spiral vegetable slicer, cut the zucchini into long thin strands, cutting through the strands with kitchen scissors to separate them for easier serving (see Note).

3. Heat the olive oil in a large skillet or wok over medium-high heat. Add the bell pepper, and cook, stirring frequently, until tender, 3 to 4 minutes.

4. Stir in the snap peas, carrots, zucchini noodles, and soy sauce mixture, and continue to cook until the zucchini is tender, 3 to 5 minutes.

5. Serve immediately, garnished with sesame seeds, if desired.

Note: If you don't have a spiral vegetable slicer, use a vegetable peeler to shave the zucchini into ribbons, discarding the seeds.

PER SERVING: CALORIES 117 FAT 5.1g PROTEIN 4g CARB 14g FIBER 3g CHOL 0mg IRON 1mg SODIUM 588mg CALC 46mg

This refreshing spiralized zucchini salad is ready in no time. For extra flavor, roast the tomatoes while you assemble the rest of your ingredients—it's a simple step, but one that makes all the difference. You can thank me later.

ZUCCHINI SALAD *with* ROASTED TOMATOES *and* MOZZARELLA

SERVES 4   PREP TIME: 15 MINUTES   TOTAL TIME: 20 MINUTES   **GF**   **VEG**

FOR THE BALSAMIC VINAIGRETTE

½ cup balsamic vinegar

⅓ cup olive oil

2 cloves garlic, crushed in a garlic press

1 tablespoon dried parsley

1 teaspoon sugar, plus more to taste

1 teaspoon dried basil

1 teaspoon dried oregano

2 cups cherry tomatoes

1 tablespoon olive oil

Kosher salt and freshly ground black pepper, to taste

2 medium zucchini (about 10 ounces each), trimmed

1 (8-ounce) container fresh mozzarella cheese pearls

¼ cup fresh basil leaves, rolled and thinly sliced into ribbons

1. Preheat the oven to 450°F. Lightly oil a baking sheet or coat it with nonstick spray.

2. Make the balsamic vinaigrette: In a large bowl, whisk together the vinegar, olive oil, garlic, parsley, sugar, basil, and oregano; set aside.

3. Arrange the tomatoes in a single layer on the prepared baking sheet. Add the olive oil and salt and pepper to taste. Gently toss to combine. Roast for 5 to 6 minutes, tossing once, until the tomatoes are blistered and beginning to burst; set aside.

4. Using a spiral vegetable slicer, cut the zucchini into long thin strands, cutting through the strands with kitchen scissors to separate them for easier serving (see Note).

5. To assemble the salad, put the zucchini strands in a large bowl; top with the roasted tomatoes, mozzarella, and basil. Pour ⅓ cup of the balsamic vinaigrette on top of the salad (reserving the remaining dressing for another use), and gently toss to combine. Serve immediately.

Note: If you don't have a spiral vegetable slicer, use a vegetable peeler to shave the zucchini into ribbons, discarding the seeds.

PER SERVING: CALORIES 318 FAT 25.6g PROTEIN 12g CARB 11g FIBER 2g CHOL 46mg IRON 1mg SODIUM 173mg CALC 46mg

This is the perfect recipe to use up all those veggies lingering in your fridge and pantry. You can use the zucchini, carrots, corn, and bell peppers in the ingredients list below or mix it up with celery, beets, mushrooms, or black beans. Just chop or grate the quantities specified in the recipe and swap them in! Avocado would also add wonderful flavor and creaminess. When you're ready to serve, you can use slider buns and your favorite sandwich spread; I like Ranch dressing with a dash of buffalo sauce!

CLEAN-OUT-THE-FRIDGE CHICKEN SLIDERS

SERVES 8 TO 10   PREP TIME: 15 MINUTES   TOTAL TIME: 23 MINUTES   KF

1 1/2 pounds ground chicken

1 red bell pepper, diced (about 1 cup)

1 small zucchini, grated (about 1 cup)

1 carrot, peeled and finely grated (about 1/2 cup)

1/2 cup corn kernels, frozen (thawed), canned, or roasted

1/2 cup Italian-style breadcrumbs

1/4 cup chopped fresh cilantro leaves

1/4 teaspoon cayenne pepper

1 large egg, lightly beaten

Juice of 1 lime

1 teaspoon kosher salt

1/4 teaspoon freshly ground black pepper

Olive oil or nonstick cooking spray

1. Preheat a gas or charcoal grill, or place a grill pan over medium-high heat.

2. In a large bowl, combine the ground chicken, bell pepper, zucchini, carrot, corn, breadcrumbs, cilantro, cayenne pepper, egg, lime juice, salt, and pepper.

3. Using a wooden spoon or a fork, gently mix the ingredients until evenly incorporated. Using your hands, shape the chicken mixture into 20 (2-inch) patties.

4. Coat the patties with a little olive oil or nonstick spray. Grill the patties until browned on the outside and cooked through, 3 to 4 minutes per side. Serve immediately.

PER SERVING: CALORIES 145 FAT 6.5g PROTEIN 14g CARB 8g FIBER 1g CHOL 77mg IRON 1mg SODIUM 338mg CALC 20mg

This scrumptious main dish is now the only way I'll have the Chinese takeout favorite orange chicken—in cauliflower form, of course. It's completely vegetarian, but don't worry—picky eaters in your household may not even notice a difference!

BATTER-FRIED CAULIFLOWER
with ORANGE SAUCE

SERVES 4   PREP TIME: 20 MINUTES   TOTAL TIME: 30 MINUTES   VEG

FOR THE ORANGE SAUCE

½ cup vegetable broth

¼ cup freshly squeezed orange juice

¼ cup sugar

2 tablespoons white vinegar

2 tablespoons reduced-sodium soy sauce

2 cloves garlic, minced

1 tablespoon orange zest

1 teaspoon Sriracha sauce, plus more to taste

1 tablespoon cornstarch whisked with 1 tablespoon water

1 head cauliflower, cut into florets

Kosher salt and freshly ground black pepper, to taste

½ cup cornstarch

2 large eggs, beaten

¼ cup vegetable oil

1 teaspoon sesame seeds, for garnish, optional

1 green onion, thinly sliced, for garnish, optional

1. Make the orange sauce: In a medium saucepan over medium heat, whisk together the vegetable broth, orange juice, sugar, vinegar, soy sauce, garlic, orange zest, and Sriracha. Bring to a boil, and stir in the cornstarch mixture. Cook, stirring frequently, until thickened 1 to 2 minutes; keep warm.

2. Put the cauliflower in a large bowl, and season with salt and pepper to taste. Stir in the cornstarch, and gently toss to coat the cauliflower. Working with one floret at a time, dip the cauliflower into the eggs; set aside on a baking sheet.

3. Heat the vegetable oil in a large saucepan over medium-high heat. Add the coated cauliflower, and cook until the florets are golden brown on all sides, 1 to 2 minutes. Transfer to a paper towel–lined plate; discard excess oil.

4. Serve the cauliflower immediately with the orange sauce, garnished with the sesame seeds and green onions, if desired.

PER SERVING: CALORIES 335 FAT 17.1g PROTEIN 7g CARB 41g FIBER 3g CHOL 93mg IRON 1mg SODIUM 567mg CALC 56mg

Bacon, eggs, and smoked salmon make for a killer salad bowl. And the dressing, a Greek yogurt Ranch, is out of this world at half the calories of the traditional mayo-and-sour cream version. Instead of hard-boiled eggs, you could also go with poached.

SMOKED SALMON COBB SALAD

SERVES 2   PREP TIME: 10 MINUTES   TOTAL TIME: 30 MINUTES   GF

FOR THE GREEK YOGURT RANCH DRESSING

1/3 cup plain Greek yogurt

1/4 cup buttermilk

1/4 teaspoon dried dill

1/4 teaspoon garlic powder

1/4 teaspoon onion powder

Kosher salt and freshly ground black pepper, to taste

4 slices bacon, diced

5 cups loosely packed baby arugula (about 3 1/2 ounces)

2 large hard-boiled eggs (see Note), diced

4 ounces thinly sliced smoked salmon, cut crosswise into 1/2-inch ribbons

1 ripe avocado, pitted, peeled, and sliced

1/2 cup corn kernels, frozen (thawed), canned, or roasted

1. Make the Greek yogurt Ranch dressing: Whisk together the yogurt, buttermilk, dill, garlic powder, and onion powder in a small bowl; season with salt and pepper to taste. Set aside.

2. Heat a large skillet over medium-high heat. Add the bacon, and cook until brown and crispy, 6 to 8 minutes. Transfer to a paper towel–lined plate; set aside.

3. To assemble the salad, put the arugula in a large bowl; arrange individual rows of the bacon, eggs, salmon, avocado, and corn. Serve immediately with the Greek yogurt Ranch dressing.

Note: To prepare hard-boiled eggs, put the eggs in a large saucepan and cover with cold water by 1 inch. Bring to a boil, and cook for 1 minute. Cover the pot with a tight-fitting lid, and remove it from the heat; set aside for 8 to 10 minutes. Drain well, and let the eggs cool before peeling and dicing.

PER SERVING: CALORIES 441 FAT 27.3g PROTEIN 28g CARB 22g FIBER 6g CHOL 222mg IRON 3mg SODIUM 991mg CALC 241mg

Incredibly simple and fast to prepare, this is one of those perfect weeknight dinners. The fish has a super-crisp crust while still boasting a wonderfully flaky interior. And the lemon cream sauce (lightened with Greek yogurt) is the ultimate guilt-free accompaniment. You can drizzle, spoon, or dip as desired.

PAN-SEARED SALMON *with* LEMON CREAM SAUCE

SERVES 4   **PREP TIME:** 10 MINUTES   **TOTAL TIME:** 25 MINUTES

FOR THE LEMON CREAM SAUCE

½ cup plain Greek yogurt

2 tablespoons mayonnaise

Juice of 1 lemon

2 cloves garlic, crushed with a garlic press

½ teaspoon dried thyme

½ teaspoon dried oregano

¼ teaspoon dried dill

Kosher salt and freshly ground black pepper, to taste

4 (5-ounce) salmon fillets

Kosher salt and freshly ground black pepper

4 tablespoons all-purpose flour

2 tablespoons unsalted butter

4 tablespoons honey

2 tablespoons chopped fresh parsley leaves, for garnish, optional

1. Preheat the oven to 400°F.

2. Make the lemon cream sauce: In a small bowl, combine the yogurt, mayonnaise, lemon juice, garlic, thyme, oregano, and dill; season with salt and pepper to taste. Set aside.

3. Season the salmon with salt and pepper. Dredge each salmon fillet in 1 tablespoon of the flour.

4. Melt the butter in a large ovenproof skillet over medium-high heat. Add the salmon to the skillet, flesh side down, and sear for 2 minutes. Turn the fillets and drizzle with the honey. Transfer the skillet to the oven, and bake the salmon until cooked through, 8 to 10 minutes (see Note).

5. Serve immediately with the lemon cream sauce. Garnish with parsley, if desired.

Note: Cooking time will vary depending on the thickness of the salmon fillets.

PER SERVING: CALORIES 484 **FAT** 28.8g **PROTEIN** 32g **CARB** 26g **FIBER** 0g **CHOL** 108mg **IRON** 2mg **SODIUM** 245mg **CALC** 104mg

My favorite thing to make for a weekend brunch with friends.

Your sides and main all in one pot!

5
QUICK-FIX SLOW COOKER

Need to put a healthy and exciting dinner on the table, night after night? Let the slow cooker do the work for you. With just 10 to 15 minutes of prep, you can throw everything into the slow cooker, leave for work, and come home to a delicious meal. Just set it and forget it.

Did you know that French toast can easily be made in your slow cooker? It's the perfect indulgence for a lazy Sunday brunch so you're not slaving away in the kitchen all morning. Don't forget to pair it with Grapefruit Mimosas (page 212)!

SLOW-COOKER FRENCH TOAST

SERVES 8   PREP TIME: 15 MINUTES   TOTAL TIME: 1 HOUR 45 MINUTES   `KF` `VEG`

FOR THE CRUMB TOPPING

¼ cup all-purpose flour

¼ cup packed brown sugar

½ teaspoon ground cinnamon

4 tablespoons unsalted butter, chilled and cut into cubes

1 (20-ounce) loaf challah, sliced

2 cups whole milk

4 large eggs

Zest of 1 lemon

1 teaspoon vanilla extract

1 teaspoon ground cinnamon

¼ teaspoon ground nutmeg

1 cup fresh blueberries

2 tablespoons confectioners' sugar, for serving, optional

¼ cup chopped toasted pecans, for serving, optional

1. Make the crumb topping: Combine the flour, sugar, and cinnamon in a small bowl. Add the cold butter, toss to coat, and then use your fingers to work the butter into the dry ingredients until the mixtures resembles coarse crumbs; set aside.

2. Lightly coat the inside of a 5- or 6-quart slow cooker with nonstick spray. Cut the challah slices in half crosswise; arrange them in the slow cooker in several layers, overlapping slightly.

3. In a large glass measuring cup or another bowl, whisk together the milk, eggs, lemon zest, vanilla, cinnamon, and nutmeg. Pour the batter evenly over the bread slices.

4. Sprinkle the crumb topping evenly over the bread slices. Top with the blueberries.

5. Cover and cook the French toast on low heat for 3 hours or on high for 1½ hours, until a knife comes out clean.

6. Serve immediately, sprinkled with confectioners' sugar and pecans, if desired.

PER SERVING: **CALORIES** 403 **FAT** 14g **PROTEIN** 13g **CARB** 56g **FIBER** 1g **CHOL** 122mg **IRON** 3mg **SODIUM** 444mg **CALC** 104mg

This vegetarian lasagna is pretty effortless. All you have to do is layer your uncooked noodles with the marinara sauce, spinach filling, and mozzarella and let the slow cooker do the work. Easy! No need to pre-boil the noodles here. You can even swap out the spinach for other veggies, if you choose.

SLOW-COOKER SPINACH LASAGNA

SERVES 8   PREP TIME: 15 MINUTES   **TOTAL TIME:** 6 HOURS 15 MINUTES   KF

1 (28-ounce) can crushed tomatoes

¼ cup fresh basil leaves, minced

1 tablespoon Worcestershire sauce

1 tablespoon sugar

1 teaspoon Italian seasoning

½ teaspoon garlic powder

Kosher salt and freshly ground black pepper, to taste

2 (10-ounce) packages frozen chopped spinach, thawed and drained

1 (15-ounce) container whole-milk ricotta cheese

½ cup freshly grated Parmesan cheese

9 lasagna noodles

2 cups shredded mozzarella cheese

2 tablespoons chopped fresh parsley leaves, for garnish, optional

1. Lightly coat the inside of a 6-quart slow cooker with nonstick spray.

2. In a large bowl, whisk together the tomatoes, basil, Worcestershire, sugar, Italian seasoning, and garlic powder; season with salt and pepper to taste. Set the marinara aside.

3. In a medium bowl, mix together the spinach, ricotta, and Parmesan; set the spinach filling aside.

4. Spread 1 cup of the marinara in the bottom of the slow cooker. Top with 3 lasagna noodles, breaking to fit if necessary. Top with half the spinach filling and ½ cup of the mozzarella. Repeat with 3 more noodles, 1 cup marinara, the remaining spinach filling, and ½ cup mozzarella. Top with the remaining 3 noodles, 1 cup marinara, and the remaining 1 cup mozzarella.

5. Cover the slow cooker, and cook the lasagna on low heat for 4 to 6 hours, or until the noodles are tender. Serve immediately, garnished with parsley, if desired.

PER SERVING: CALORIES 381 **FAT** 16.7g **PROTEIN** 24g **CARB** 35g **FIBER** 5g **CHOL** 47mg **IRON** 4mg **SODIUM** 682mg **CALC** 542mg

Homemade chicken stock is the perfect way to repurpose leftover chicken bones and carcass, along with all those lingering veggies in your fridge. But don't worry, the slow cooker does all the work for you. Just set the timer and walk away, literally, for 12 to 18 hours. I like to have plenty on hand, especially when soup and stew season starts in the fall, because at the end of the day, a box of stock doesn't even compare to homemade.

SLOW-COOKER CHICKEN STOCK

MAKES 6 CUPS   **PREP TIME:** 10 MINUTES   **TOTAL TIME:** 18 HOURS   `GF`

1 whole chicken carcass or leftover chicken bones

1 large onion, quartered

2 parsnips, chopped

3 stalks celery, chopped

3 carrots, chopped

3 cloves garlic

1 tablespoon black peppercorns

3 bay leaves

2 sprigs fresh rosemary

2 sprigs fresh thyme

1 sprig fresh dill

7 cups water

Kosher salt and freshly ground black pepper, to taste

1. Place the chicken, onion, parsnips, celery, carrots, garlic, peppercorns, bay leaves, rosemary, thyme, and dill into a 6-quart slow cooker. Stir in 7 cups water until well combined; season with salt and pepper to taste.

2. Cover and cook on low heat for 12 to 18 hours; let cool, and strain, discarding vegetables and herbs.

3. Store in airtight containers in the refrigerator for 3 to 4 days or in the freezer for up to 3 months.

PER SERVING: CALORIES 10 **FAT** 0g **PROTEIN** 1g **CARB** 1g **FIBER** 0g **CHOL** 0mg **IRON** 0mg **SODIUM** 160mg **CALC** 0mg

If you're ever in the mood for cheesy enchiladas without the work of rolling, wrapping, and baking, then this recipe is for you. It offers all the creamy goodness and flavor of enchiladas but is made much more conveniently. Simply throw everything but the orzo in the slow cooker, set the time and temperature before heading out for the day, and add the pasta 30 minutes before serving time. If you want to go all out, top this off with sour cream, salsa, avocado, or a combination.

SLOW-COOKER ENCHILADA ORZO

SERVES 6 (8 TO 12 AS A SIDE)   **PREP TIME:** 10 MINUTES   **TOTAL TIME:** 8 HOURS 40 MINUTES   `KF` `VEG`

1 (14.5-ounce) can fire-roasted diced tomatoes

1 (10-ounce) can enchilada sauce

1 (4.5-ounce) can chopped green chiles, drained

1 1/2 cups vegetable broth, plus more as needed

1 (15.25-ounce) can corn kernels, drained

1 (15-ounce) can black beans, drained and rinsed

4 ounces cream cheese, cut into cubes

2 cups dried orzo (pasta shaped like a large grain of rice)

1/2 teaspoon kosher salt

1/4 teaspoon freshly ground black pepper

2 tablespoons chopped fresh cilantro leaves, for garnish, optional

1. Put the diced tomatoes and their juices, the enchilada sauce, green chiles, 1/2 cup of the vegetable broth, the corn, and black beans into a 5- or 6-quart slow cooker; stir until well combined. Top with the cubes of cream cheese.

2. Cover the slow cooker, and cook on low heat for 7 to 8 hours or on high heat for 3 to 4 hours.

3. Uncover, and stir the tomato mixture until the cream cheese is well combined. Stir in the orzo and the remaining 1 cup broth. Cover and cook on high heat for 30 minutes more, stirring after 15 minutes. Add more vegetable broth as needed until the desired consistency is reached. Season with salt and pepper.

4. Serve immediately, garnished with the cilantro, if desired.

PER SERVING: CALORIES 461 **FAT** 8.6g **PROTEIN** 16g **CARB** 80g **FIBER** 11g **CHOL** 21mg **IRON** 4mg **SODIUM** 1413mg **CALC** 77mg

These burrito bowls are the perfect solution for those times you need a Chipotle fix, but you get much more chicken when you make them at home. This recipe is enough to feed a crowd, so if you live in a small household, be prepared to enjoy this all week. You can serve this with sour cream, shredded lettuce, or salsa, if you choose.

SLOW-COOKER CHICKEN BURRITO BOWLS

SERVES 6   PREP TIME: 15 MINUTES   TOTAL TIME: 6 HOURS 30 MINUTES   KF

1 pound boneless, skinless chicken breasts

2 cups chicken stock

1 (14.5-ounce) can fire-roasted diced tomatoes

1 (4.5-ounce) can chopped green chiles, drained

1 canned chipotle chile in adobo sauce, plus 1 tablespoon sauce

2 cloves garlic, minced

1 1/2 teaspoons chili powder

1 teaspoon ground cumin

1 teaspoon dried oregano

1/2 teaspoon cayenne pepper

Kosher salt and freshly ground black pepper, to taste

1 cup long-grain white rice (see Note)

1 (15-ounce) can black beans, drained and rinsed

1 (15-ounce) can whole-kernel corn, drained

1 cup shredded Cheddar cheese

1 Roma tomato, diced, for garnish, optional

2 tablespoons chopped fresh cilantro leaves, for garnish, optional

1. Put the chicken breasts in a 6-quart slow cooker. Add 1 cup of the chicken stock, the fire-roasted tomatoes and their juices, the chiles, chipotle chile and adobo sauce, the garlic, chili powder, cumin, oregano, and cayenne pepper, and stir to combine. Season with salt and pepper to taste.

2. Cover the slow cooker, and cook on low heat for 3 to 4 hours or on high for 1 to 2 hours. Remove the chicken breasts to a cutting board, shred the meat, and return the shredded chicken to the pot with its juices.

3. Stir in the rice, black beans, corn, and remaining 1 cup chicken stock. Cover the pot, and cook on high heat for 1 to 2 hours, or until the rice is tender.

4. Top with the Cheddar. Cover and cook until the cheese has melted, 10 to 15 minutes.

5. Transfer the chicken and bean mixture to bowls, and serve immediately, garnished with the fresh tomato and cilantro, if desired, and other toppings of your choice.

Note: You can substitute 2 to 3 cups instant rice for quicker cooking—30 to 45 minutes on high heat, or until the rice is tender. Or swap in brown rice for a more wholesome bowl.

PER SERVING: CALORIES 391 FAT 8.5g PROTEIN 30g CARB 48g FIBER 8g CHOL 63mg IRON 3mg SODIUM 1112mg CALC 202mg

This is one of those surefire tried-and-true recipes that you can make any time, 365 days a year if you choose. Rain or shine, winter or summer, all it takes is 10 minutes to prep everything. Then press cook and voilà, you get a hearty, comforting meal for everyone to enjoy. So easy. So good. Many of the Damn Delicious readers have told me this is now their all-time favorite slow-cooker recipe.

SLOW-COOKER HONEY-GARLIC CHICKEN *and* VEGGIES

SERVES 4   PREP TIME: 10 MINUTES   TOTAL TIME: 8 HOURS 10 MINUTES   `KF`

FOR THE HONEY-GARLIC SAUCE

½ cup reduced-sodium soy sauce

½ cup honey

¼ cup ketchup

2 cloves garlic, minced

1 teaspoon dried basil

½ teaspoon dried oregano

¼ teaspoon crushed red pepper flakes

¼ teaspoon freshly ground black pepper

8 bone-in, skin-on chicken thighs (see Note)

1 pound baby red potatoes, halved

1 pound baby carrots

1 pound green beans, trimmed

2 tablespoons chopped fresh parsley leaves, for garnish, optional

1. Make the honey-garlic sauce: In a large bowl, combine the soy sauce, honey, ketchup, garlic, basil, oregano, red pepper flakes, and black pepper.

2. Put the chicken thighs, potatoes, carrots, green beans, and honey-garlic sauce in a 6-quart slow cooker, stirring to coat with sauce. Cover and cook on low heat for 7 to 8 hours or on high for 3 to 4 hours, basting once every hour.

3. Serve the chicken immediately, with the potatoes, carrots, and green beans. Garnish with the parsley, if desired.

Note: If you like your chicken with a crispy skin, you can quickly broil it before adding it to the slow cooker. Preheat the oven to broil. Arrange the chicken thighs on a baking sheet, skin side up, and broil until crisp, 3 to 4 minutes.

PER SERVING: **CALORIES** 502 **FAT** 7.3g **PROTEIN** 35g **CARB** 78g **FIBER** 8g **CHOL** 110mg **IRON** 5mg **SODIUM** 1527mg **CALC** 98mg

This recipe is great for beginners and lazy cooks alike. That's right, both the main and side are made together, smothered in real maple syrup, two types of mustard, and a little bit of orange zest. It's convenient—and delicious.

SLOW-COOKER MAPLE DIJON CHICKEN *and* BROCCOLI

SERVES 4   PREP TIME: 10 MINUTES   TOTAL TIME: 6 HOURS 20 MINUTES   **KF**

FOR THE MAPLE DIJON SAUCE

⅓ cup pure maple syrup

3 tablespoons Dijon mustard

1 tablespoon whole-grain mustard

1 tablespoon red wine vinegar

2 cloves garlic, minced

½ teaspoon dried rosemary

½ teaspoon dried oregano

Zest of 1 orange (see Note)

Kosher salt and freshly ground black pepper, to taste

8 teaspoons brown sugar

8 bone-in, skin-on chicken thighs

Kosher salt and freshly ground black pepper, to taste

2 tablespoons unsalted butter

2 heads broccoli, cut into florets (see Note)

2 tablespoons chopped fresh parsley leaves, for garnish, optional

1. Make the maple Dijon sauce: In a medium bowl, whisk together the maple syrup, both mustards, the vinegar, garlic, rosemary, oregano, and orange zest. Season with salt and pepper to taste; set aside.

2. Using your fingers, work the brown sugar, about 1 teaspoon per thigh, onto both sides of the chicken. Season with salt and pepper to taste.

3. Melt the butter in a large ovenproof skillet over medium-high heat. Add the chicken thighs, starting with skin side down, and sear both sides until golden brown, 2 to 3 minutes per side.

4. Transfer the seared chicken thighs to a 6-quart slow cooker. Stir in the maple Dijon sauce. Cover and cook on low heat for 5 to 6 hours or on high for 2 to 3 hours. Add the broccoli florets during the last 30 minutes of cooking time.

5. Serve the chicken and broccoli immediately with plenty of the sauce. Garnish with the parsley, if desired.

Note: Lemon zest can be substituted for the orange zest, or use a combination. Brussels sprouts can be substituted for the broccoli.

PER SERVING: CALORIES 366 **FAT** 12.3g **PROTEIN** 31g **CARB** 35g **FIBER** 3g **CHOL** 125mg **IRON** 2mg **SODIUM** 704mg **CALC** 79mg

Set your slow cooker right before you leave for work so you can come home to the most tender, melt-in-your-mouth French dip sandwiches. The meat, slow-cooked for 8 hours, becomes moist, tender, and packed with maximum flavor. The leftover au jus can come in handy for gravies or beef stews!

SLOW-COOKER FRENCH DIP SANDWICHES

SERVES 8   PREP TIME: 15 MINUTES   TOTAL TIME: 8 HOURS 20 MINUTES   KF

2 cups beef broth

¼ cup balsamic vinegar

2 tablespoons Worcestershire sauce

2 tablespoons reduced-sodium soy sauce

1 teaspoon dried rosemary

1 teaspoon dried thyme

1 teaspoon Sriracha sauce, optional

1 (3-pound) boneless beef chuck roast, trimmed

2 onions, thinly sliced

4 cloves garlic, peeled and left whole

1 bay leaf

8 mini (5-inch) baguettes or sandwich buns, split lengthwise

8 slices provolone cheese, halved

1. In a large bowl, whisk together the beef broth, balsamic vinegar, Worcestershire sauce, soy sauce, rosemary, thyme, and Sriracha.

2. Put the chuck roast in a 5- or 6-quart slow cooker. Add the beef broth mixture along with the onions, garlic cloves, and bay leaf.

3. Cover the slow cooker, and cook on low heat for 7 to 8 hours or on high heat for 3 to 4 hours.

4. Preheat the oven to 450°F. Transfer the roast to a cutting board and thinly slice it against the grain, reserving the beef broth mixture. Remove and reserve the onions from the broth mixture, and skim the fat from the surface.

5. Arrange the baguettes or sandwich buns, cut sides up, on a baking sheet. Bake until the bread is lightly toasted, 2 to 3 minutes.

6. To serve, fill the baguettes with beef and the reserved onions, if desired. Top with the cheese slices, and return to the oven until the cheese has melted, about 2 minutes more.

7. Serve immediately with the beef broth mixture for dipping.

PER SERVING: CALORIES 652 FAT 34.3g PROTEIN 51g CARB 33g FIBER 3g CHOL 168mg IRON 5mg SODIUM 755mg CALC 270mg

This low and slow recipe transforms budget-friendly chuck roast into an almost effortless, tender Korean beef. Serve it on a bed of rice, wrap it in lettuce, or serve it in tacos. You can also use the leftover sauce as a condiment for plain white rice.

SLOW-COOKER KOREAN BEEF

SERVES 8   **PREP TIME:** 10 MINUTES   **TOTAL TIME:** 8 HOURS 40 MINUTES

1 cup beef broth

½ cup reduced-sodium soy sauce

½ cup packed brown sugar

4 cloves garlic, minced

1 tablespoon sesame oil

1 tablespoon rice wine vinegar

1 tablespoon freshly grated ginger

1 teaspoon Sriracha sauce, plus more to taste

½ teaspoon onion powder

½ teaspoon ground white pepper

1 (3-pound) boneless beef chuck roast, cut into 1-inch cubes

2 tablespoons cornstarch

¼ cup water

2 green onions, thinly sliced, for garnish, optional

1 teaspoon sesame seeds, for garnish, optional

1. In a large bowl, whisk together the beef broth, soy sauce, brown sugar, garlic, oil, vinegar, ginger, Sriracha, onion powder, and white pepper.

2. Put the chuck roast in a 5- or 6-quart slow cooker. Stir in the beef broth mixture until well combined.

3. Cover and cook on low heat for 7 to 8 hours or on high heat for 3 to 4 hours, or until the cubes of meat are very tender but still retain their shape.

4. In a small bowl, whisk together the cornstarch and ¼ cup water. Stir the mixture into the broth in the slow cooker. Cover and cook on high heat for an additional 30 minutes, or until the sauce has thickened.

5. Serve immediately, garnished with the green onions and sesame seeds, if desired.

PER SERVING: CALORIES 482 **FAT** 26.3g **PROTEIN** 40g **CARB** 19g **FIBER** 0g **CHOL** 153mg **IRON** 3mg **SODIUM** 700mg **CALC** 40mg

TIP
This high-protein, high-iron, low-fat dish is a perfect choice for anyone looking to boost their iron intake.

This only takes 6 minutes to prep.

A must for date night. All you need is 5 ingredients. E-A-S-Y

6

30-MINUTE SUPPER SPRINTS

Yes, big flavor can happen in minutes! These easy-to-execute recipes prove that making an amazing home-cooked meal every night is totally achievable. Ready? Go!

Linguine con vongole is a simple pasta dish with sophistication and elegance, making it a great date-night or dinner-party meal. Your guests don't have to know how easy (and affordable) this dish really is!

EASY LINGUINE WITH CLAMS

SERVES 4   PREP TIME: 5 MINUTES   TOTAL TIME: 20 MINUTES

12 ounces dried linguine

3 tablespoons unsalted butter

2 tablespoons minced garlic (about 6 cloves)

⅛ teaspoon crushed red pepper flakes, optional

½ cup chicken broth, plus more as needed

Kosher salt and freshly ground black pepper, to taste

2 pounds littleneck clams, cleaned

2 tablespoons chopped fresh parsley leaves, for garnish, optional

1. In a large pot of boiling salted water, cook the pasta according to package instructions; drain well, reserving ½ cup of the pasta water.

2. Meanwhile, melt the butter in a large saucepan over medium-high heat. Add the garlic and red pepper flakes, if desired, and cook, stirring frequently, until fragrant, about 1 minute. Stir in the chicken broth; season with salt and pepper to taste.

3. Bring the broth mixture to a boil; reduce the heat and simmer until reduced by half, about 5 minutes. Stir in the clams. Cover with a tight-fitting lid, and cook until the clams have opened, 5 to 8 minutes. Discard any unopened clams.

4. Stir in the pasta and the reserved pasta water, 1 tablespoon at a time, as needed.

5. Serve immediately, garnished with the parsley, if desired.

PER SERVING: CALORIES 475 FAT 10.9g PROTEIN 20g CARB 67g FIBER 3g CHOL 46mg IRON 4mg SODIUM 681mg CALC 48mg

All you need is five ingredients and five minutes prep time to make the easiest pasta of all time. This creamy main dish, loaded with freshly grated Parmesan and crisp bacon goodness, is one of my all-time favorites. If you are tempted to use the Parmesan cheese that comes in a green can, I advise against it. Fresh Parmesan is always best!

SPAGHETTI CARBONARA

SERVES 4   PREP TIME: 5 MINUTES   TOTAL TIME: 20 MINUTES   KF

8 ounces dried spaghetti

2 large eggs

$3/4$ cup freshly grated Parmesan cheese

4 slices bacon, diced

4 cloves garlic, minced

$3/4$ teaspoon kosher salt

$1/2$ teaspoon freshly ground black pepper

2 tablespoons chopped fresh parsley leaves, for garnish, optional

TIP

To dice uncooked bacon, I recommend putting it in the freezer for 10 to 15 minutes first. The colder the bacon, the easier to slice and dice!

1. In a large pot of boiling salted water, cook the pasta according to package instructions; drain well, reserving $1/2$ cup of the pasta water.

2. Meanwhile, in a small bowl, whisk together the eggs and Parmesan; set aside.

3. Heat a large skillet over medium-high heat. Add the bacon, and cook until browned and crispy, 6 to 8 minutes; discard excess fat.

4. Add the garlic, and stir until fragrant, about 1 minute. Reduce the heat to low.

5. Working quickly, add the pasta and the egg mixture to the skillet, and gently toss to combine; season with salt and pepper. Stir in the reserved pasta water, 1 tablespoon at a time, until desired consistency is reached.

6. Serve immediately, garnished with the parsley, if desired.

PER SERVING: CALORIES 365 **FAT** 11.1g **PROTEIN** 21g **CARB** 43g **FIBER** 2g **CHOL** 111mg **IRON** 2mg **SODIUM** 599mg **CALC** 323mg

This is a super-speedy supper made with homemade pesto. If you're really in a hurry, you can shave off another five minutes by using store-bought pesto, but aren't you worth the extra effort?

PESTO PASTA

SERVES 4   PREP TIME: 10 MINUTES   TOTAL TIME: 20 MINUTES

FOR THE PESTO

1 cup loosely packed fresh basil leaves (see Note)

3 cloves garlic, peeled and left whole

3 tablespoons pine nuts

$1/3$ cup freshly grated Parmesan cheese

Kosher salt and freshly ground black pepper, to taste

$1/3$ cup olive oil

8 ounces dried rotini

2 cups cherry tomatoes, cut in half

2 cups loosely packed baby arugula (see Note)

$1/4$ cup freshly grated Parmesan cheese

$1/4$ cup pine nuts

1. Make the pesto: Puree the basil, garlic, pine nuts, and Parmesan in the bowl of a food processor; season with salt and pepper to taste. With the motor running, add the olive oil in a slow stream until emulsified; set aside.

2. In a large pot of boiling salted water, cook the pasta according to package instructions; drain well.

3. In a large bowl, combine the pasta, $1/2$ cup of the pesto (see Note), tomatoes, arugula, Parmesan, and pine nuts, tossing to thoroughly combine. Serve immediately.

Note: Spinach or kale can be substituted for the basil and/or the arugula. The leftover pesto can be stored in an airtight container in the refrigerator for up to 1 week.

PER SERVING: CALORIES 550 FAT 33.2g PROTEIN 17g CARB 48g FIBER 4g CHOL 12mg IRON 3mg SODIUM 421mg CALC 289mg

Okay, so here's the deal: Make this chicken over the weekend and your weekday meals are virtually done. I cook up a batch of this chicken on Sunday and use it throughout the week to throw into salads, quesadillas, pastas, sandwiches, soups—you name it. It's a no-fail timesaver!

ALL-PURPOSE CHICKEN

SERVES 4   PREP TIME: 10 MINUTES   TOTAL TIME: 30 MINUTES   GF   KF

2 pounds boneless, skinless chicken breasts, cut into ½-inch strips

2 tablespoons olive oil

2 tablespoons freshly squeezed lemon juice

1 teaspoon dried basil

1 teaspoon dried oregano

1 teaspoon dried thyme

¼ teaspoon cayenne pepper

2 cloves garlic, minced

Kosher salt and freshly ground black pepper

2 tablespoons chopped fresh parsley leaves, for garnish, optional

1 tablespoon lemon rind, for garnish, optional

1. Preheat the oven to 400°F (see Note).

2. Place chicken in a single layer onto a baking sheet. Add the oil, lemon juice, basil, oregano, thyme, cayenne pepper, and garlic. Season with salt and pepper. Gently toss to combine.

3. Bake for 15 to 18 minutes, or until the chicken is no longer pink in the center.

4. Serve immediately, garnished with parsley and lemon rind, if desired. To store, refrigerate or freeze in an airtight container within 1 to 2 hours of cooking.

Note: Alternatively, you can grill the chicken over medium-high heat.

PER SERVING: CALORIES 347 FAT 12.7g PROTEIN 57g CARB 2g FIBER 0g CHOL 193mg IRON 1mg SODIUM 219mg CALC 26mg

TIP

You can store cooked chicken in an airtight container in the refrigerator for up to 4 days or in the freezer for 3 to 4 months.

This may just be my favorite pasta dish yet. It is a quick weeknight recipe that uses fresh, simple ingredients you probably already have on hand. The tomatoes and basil are key here. The juices from the tomatoes coupled with the melted butter make a fantastic sauce for the fettucine.

TOMATO BASIL CHICKEN FETTUCINE

SERVES 4   PREP TIME: 10 MINUTES   TOTAL TIME: 30 MINUTES   KF

8 ounces dried fettucine (see Note)

2 boneless, skinless chicken breasts

1 tablespoon Italian seasoning

Kosher salt and freshly ground black pepper

1 tablespoon olive oil

2 cloves garlic, minced

2 cups cherry tomatoes, halved

1 cup fresh basil leaves, chiffonade

½ teaspoon crushed red pepper flakes, optional

½ cup unsalted butter

Kosher salt and freshly ground black pepper, to taste

¼ cup freshly grated Parmesan cheese

1. In a large pot of boiling salted water, cook the pasta according to package instructions; drain well.

2. Meanwhile, season the chicken with Italian seasoning, salt, and pepper.

3. Heat the olive oil in a large skillet over medium-high heat. Add the chicken, and cook through, 5 to 6 minutes per side. Place chicken on a plate, and keep warm.

4. Add the garlic, tomatoes, basil, and red pepper flakes to the skillet. Cook, stirring occasionally, until tomatoes begin to burst and soften, about 5 minutes.

5. Stir in the pasta and butter until melted and well combined, about 2 minutes; season with salt and pepper to taste.

6. Serve immediately, topped with chicken and garnished with the Parmesan.

Note: Spaghetti or linguine can be substituted for the fettucine.

PER SERVING: CALORIES 775 FAT 35.6g PROTEIN 68g CARB 46g FIBER 3g CHOL 259mg IRON 4mg SODIUM 350mg CALC 158mg

Use thin-sliced chicken cutlets to make this quick dish in less than 20 minutes. If your local grocery store does not carry this cut of chicken, you can easily prepare your own using boneless, skinless chicken breasts (see step 2), which can actually save you up to $2 per pound.

GREEK CHICKEN

SERVES 4   PREP TIME: 10 MINUTES   TOTAL TIME: 16 MINUTES   GF

2 boneless, skinless chicken breasts

½ teaspoon kosher salt

¼ teaspoon freshly ground black pepper

2 tablespoons olive oil

2 cups cherry tomatoes, cut in half

1 Persian cucumber, diced

½ cup canned pitted Kalamata olives, drained and sliced

¼ cup chopped red onion

2 cloves garlic, crushed with a garlic press

1 tablespoon freshly squeezed lemon juice

½ teaspoon dried oregano

2 tablespoons chopped fresh parsley leaves

Kosher salt and freshly ground black pepper, to taste

¼ cup crumbled feta

1. Preheat a gas or charcoal grill, or place a grill pan over medium-high heat.

2. Put 1 chicken breast on a cutting board. With your hand flat on top of it, carefully slice the chicken in half horizontally. Trim excess fat as needed. Repeat with the other chicken breast. Season with ½ teaspoon salt and ¼ teaspoon pepper. Brush with 1 tablespoon of the olive oil.

3. Add the chicken to the grill or grill pan, and cook until browned and cooked through, 2 to 3 minutes per side.

4. In a large bowl, combine the tomatoes, cucumber, olives, onion, garlic, remaining olive oil, lemon juice, oregano, and parsley; season with salt and pepper to taste.

5. Serve chicken immediately, topped with the tomato mixture and the feta.

PER SERVING: CALORIES 281 **FAT** 13.5g **PROTEIN** 33g **CARB** 9g **FIBER** 2g **CHOL** 110mg **IRON** 2mg **SODIUM** 488mg **CALC** 85mg

When you need to get a meal on the table quickly, this is the way to go. You bake everything in the same pan, letting the juice from the honey-Dijon pork chops drizzle onto your veggies as it all gets roasted to crisp perfection. Boom.

PORK CHOPS *with* ASPARAGUS, TOMATOES, *and* CORN

SERVES 4   PREP TIME: 10 MINUTES   TOTAL TIME: 30 MINUTES   KF

4 tablespoons olive oil

2 tablespoons honey

1 tablespoon Dijon mustard

2 cloves garlic, minced

½ teaspoon dried thyme

1 teaspoon kosher salt

½ teaspoon freshly ground black pepper

4 (8-ounce) bone-in pork chops, 1 inch thick, patted dry

1 pound asparagus spears, trimmed

2 cups cherry tomatoes

2 cups corn, frozen (thawed), canned, or roasted

2 tablespoons chopped fresh parsley leaves, for garnish, optional

1. Preheat the oven to 400°F.

2. In a small bowl, whisk together 2 tablespoons olive oil, the honey, Dijon, garlic, thyme, and ½ teaspoon salt and ¼ teaspoon pepper. Brush each pork chop with the honey-Dijon mixture.

3. Heat an ovensafe grill pan over medium-high heat. Add the pork chops, and sear both sides until golden brown, about 2 minutes per side; set aside.

4. Add the remaining 2 tablespoons olive oil, the asparagus, tomatoes, and corn to the pan; season with the remaining ½ teaspoon salt and ¼ teaspoon pepper. Gently toss to combine. Place the pork chops on top of the vegetables in the pan. Transfer the pan to the oven, and roast until the pork chops are completely cooked through, 8 to 10 minutes (see Note). Remove the pork to a platter; return the pan with the vegetables to the oven, and cook for 5 minutes more, or until the asparagus is tender.

5. Top the chops with the veggies and sauce, and serve immediately, garnished with the parsley, if desired.

Note: Cooking time will vary depending on the size and thickness of the pork chops. They're done when a meat thermometer inserted horizontally into the center of a chop reads 140°F.

PER SERVING: CALORIES 412 FAT 24.7g PROTEIN 31g CARB 17g FIBER 3g CHOL 89mg IRON 4mg SODIUM 663mg CALC 101mg

The secret to cooking juicy, tender pork chops is to give them a good sear in melted butter and then finish them off in the oven. If you don't have an ovenproof skillet handy, transfer the pork chops to a baking dish to roast. Don't be surprised if you're tempted to ditch the pork chops and guzzle down the glaze instead—it's that good.

PORK CHOPS with SWEET and SOUR GLAZE

SERVES 4   PREP TIME: 5 MINUTES   TOTAL TIME: 18 MINUTES   GF   KF

4 (8-ounce) bone-in pork chops, 3/4 to 1 inch thick, patted dry

Kosher salt and freshly ground black pepper, to taste

2 tablespoons unsalted butter

FOR THE SWEET AND SOUR GLAZE

1/4 cup balsamic vinegar

3 tablespoons honey

2 cloves garlic, minced

1/2 teaspoon dried oregano

1/2 teaspoon dried basil

1/2 teaspoon dried thyme

Pinch of crushed red pepper flakes, optional

Kosher salt and freshly ground black pepper, to taste

1. Preheat the oven to 400°F.

2. Season the pork chops with salt and pepper to taste.

3. Melt the butter in a large ovenproof skillet over medium-high heat. Sear one side of the pork chops until golden brown, 2 to 3 minutes. Flip the chops, and transfer to the oven.

4. Roast the chops until completely cooked through, 8 to 10 minutes (see Note).

5. Meanwhile, make the sweet and sour glaze: In a small saucepan over medium heat, whisk together the vinegar, honey, garlic, oregano, basil, thyme, and red pepper flakes, if desired. Season with salt and pepper to taste. Bring the sauce to a boil; reduce the heat to medium-low, and simmer until slightly thickened, about 5 minutes.

6. Serve the pork chops immediately, drizzled with the sweet and sour glaze.

Note: Cooking time will vary depending on the size and thickness of the pork chops. They're done when a meat thermometer inserted horizontally into the center of a chop reads 140°F.

PER SERVING: CALORIES 336 FAT 16.7g PROTEIN 29g CARB 17g FIBER 0g CHOL 104mg IRON 2mg SODIUM 332mg CALC 80mg

You know what's good about this recipe? Everything. It's great exactly as is, but it's also flexible enough to add variations. Try swapping out the pork chops for thin-sliced chicken breasts, the cremini mushrooms for white buttons, and the spinach for kale.

PORK MARSALA *with* MUSHROOMS *and* SPINACH

SERVES 4   PREP TIME: 10 MINUTES   TOTAL TIME: 25 MINUTES

4 (5-ounce) boneless pork chops, about ¾ inch thick, patted dry

½ teaspoon kosher salt

¼ teaspoon freshly ground black pepper

¼ cup all-purpose flour

3 tablespoons unsalted butter

2 cloves garlic, minced

1 shallot, diced

8 ounces cremini mushrooms, thinly sliced

1 tablespoon all-purpose flour

½ cup dry Marsala wine

½ cup chicken stock

½ teaspoon dried thyme

2 tablespoons heavy cream

2 cups loosely packed baby spinach

Kosher salt and freshly ground black pepper, to taste

2 tablespoons chopped fresh parsley leaves, for garnish, optional

1. Season the pork chops with the salt and pepper.

2. Working one at a time, dredge the pork chops in ¼ cup flour to coat.

3. Melt 2 tablespoons of the butter in a large skillet over medium-high heat. Add the pork chops, and sear until golden brown, about 3 minutes per side; transfer to a plate, and set aside.

4. Melt the remaining 1 tablespoon butter in the skillet. Add the garlic, shallot, and mushrooms to the skillet. Cook, stirring occasionally, until tender, about 3 minutes.

5. Whisk in 1 tablespoon flour until lightly browned, about 1 minute. Whisk in the Marsala, chicken stock, and thyme. Cook, whisking constantly, until the sauce has thickened, about 2 minutes.

6. Stir in the heavy cream and spinach until the spinach begins to wilt, 1 to 2 minutes; season with salt and pepper to taste.

7. Return the pork chops to the skillet, and cook until heated through, about 1 minute.

8. Serve immediately, garnished with the parsley, if desired.

PER SERVING: CALORIES 396 FAT 20.5g PROTEIN 27g CARB 18g FIBER 2g CHOL 105mg IRON 3mg SODIUM 595mg CALC 111mg

Just marinate your pork chops in this quick homemade BBQ sauce before leaving for work. Then you can throw them onto the grill the minute you get home. Done. Dinner ready in 10 minutes.

HONEY BBQ RANCH PORK CHOPS

SERVES 4   PREP TIME: 10 MINUTES   TOTAL TIME: 20 MINUTES PLUS MARINATING   KF

FOR THE BBQ SAUCE

¾ cup ketchup

2 tablespoons packed light brown sugar

2 tablespoons honey

1 tablespoon Worcestershire sauce

1 tablespoon Dijon mustard

1 teaspoon smoked paprika

½ teaspoon garlic powder

Freshly ground black pepper, to taste

4 (8-ounce) bone-in pork chops, ¾ to 1 inch thick, patted dry

1 (1-ounce) package Ranch Seasoning and Salad Dressing mix

2 tablespoons chopped fresh parsley leaves, for garnish, optional

1. Make the BBQ sauce: In a small bowl, whisk together the ketchup, brown sugar, honey, Worcestershire, Dijon, paprika, and garlic powder; season with pepper, to taste. Reserve ¼ cup, and set aside.

2. Season the pork chops with Ranch Seasoning.

3. In a gallon-sized zip-top bag or large bowl, combine the BBQ sauce and pork chops; marinate for at least 1 hour to overnight, turning the bag occasionally. Drain the pork chops from the marinade.

4. Preheat a gas or charcoal grill, or place a grill pan over medium-high heat.

5. Add the pork chops to the grill, and cook, flipping once and basting with reserved ¼ cup marinade until cooked through, 5 to 6 minutes on each side (see Note). Serve the pork chops immediately, drizzled with the sweet and sour glaze and garnished with parsley, if desired.

Note: Cooking time will vary depending on the size and thickness of the pork chops. They're done when a meat thermometer inserted horizontally into the center of a chop reads 140°F.

PER SERVING: CALORIES 699 FAT 26.8g PROTEIN 44g CARB 32g FIBER 0g CHOL 145mg IRON 2mg SODIUM 1745mg CALC 255mg

This salmon and salsa entrée delivers the perfect combination of sweet and savory goodness, and you can even add in a little bit of jalapeño heat for a trifecta of flavors. If you find yourself with leftover strawberry mango salsa, it makes a great dip for tortilla chips—in my experience, a welcome snack during the 10 PM to 2 AM hours.

BALSAMIC SALMON *with* STRAWBERRY MANGO SALSA

SERVES 4   PREP TIME: 10 MINUTES   TOTAL TIME: 25 MINUTES

FOR THE STRAWBERRY MANGO SALSA

¾ cup strawberries, diced

1 small ripe mango, diced (about ¾ cup)

2 tablespoons finely chopped red onion

2 tablespoons chopped fresh cilantro leaves

2 teaspoons honey, plus more to taste

Juice of 1 lime

1 jalapeño chile, seeded and minced, optional

¼ cup balsamic vinegar

2 cloves garlic, minced

1 tablespoon honey

1 tablespoon Dijon mustard

Kosher salt and freshly ground black pepper, to taste

4 (5-ounce) salmon fillets, about 1½ inches thick

1. Preheat the oven to 400°F. Lightly oil a 9- x 13-inch baking dish or coat it with nonstick spray.

2. Make the strawberry mango salsa: In a large bowl, combine the strawberries, mango, red onion, cilantro, honey, lime juice, and jalapeño, if desired; set aside.

3. In a small bowl, whisk together the vinegar, garlic, honey, and Dijon mustard; season with salt and pepper to taste.

4. Arrange the salmon in a single layer in the prepared baking dish, and brush each fillet with the balsamic mixture.

5. Roast until the fish flakes easily with a fork, brushing two to three times with the balsamic mixture, 10 to 12 minutes total (see Note).

6. Serve the salmon immediately with the strawberry mango salsa.

Note: Cooking time will vary depending on the size and thickness of the salmon fillets.

PER SERVING: CALORIES 323 FAT 15.4g PROTEIN 26g CARB 19g FIBER 1g CHOL 71mg IRON 1mg SODIUM 281mg CALC 32mg

Preparing salmon in foil is not only the easiest way to cook it, but it also seals in all the flavor with almost no work on your part. And with this blend of Cajun spices, brown sugar, and orange zest, there's just enough heat and sweetness in every bite—a winning combination anytime.

CAJUN SALMON IN FOIL

SERVE 4   PREP TIME: 10 MINUTES   TOTAL TIME: 25 MINUTES

3 tablespoons olive oil

2 tablespoons Cajun seasoning

2 tablespoons light brown sugar

2 cloves garlic, minced

Zest of 1 orange

Kosher salt and freshly ground black pepper, to taste

2 pounds salmon

2 tablespoons chopped fresh parsley leaves, for garnish, optional

TIP

Salmon is one of the top sources of omega-3 fatty acids, which are important for healthy skin, brain, and cardiovascular system.

1. Preheat the oven to 375°F. Line a baking sheet with foil.

2. In a small bowl, whisk together the olive oil, Cajun seasoning, sugar, garlic, and orange zest; season with salt and pepper to taste.

3. Place the salmon on the prepared baking sheet, and fold up all four sides of the foil. Spoon the Cajun mixture over the salmon. Fold the sides of the foil over the salmon to cover it completely, and seal the packet closed.

4. Bake until the salmon is cooked through, 15 to 20 minutes (see Note).

5. Serve immediately, garnished with the parsley, if desired.

Note: Baking time may need to be adjusted depending on the thickness of the salmon.

PER SERVING: CALORIES 465 FAT 31.1g PROTEIN 38g CARB 7g FIBER 0g CHOL 107mg IRON 1mg SODIUM 914mg CALC 29mg

Did I mention I love a good foil-packet dinner? Just season, wrap, and grill. Here, the packets seal in all the garlic-buttery juices, keeping the shrimp amazingly moist and tender. All this dish needs is 10 minutes of prep plus grill time—and zero cleanup.

GARLIC BUTTER SHRIMP IN FOIL

SERVES 4   PREP TIME: 10 MINUTES   TOTAL TIME: 18 MINUTES

4 tablespoons unsalted butter, melted

3 cloves garlic, minced

Juice of 1 lemon, plus more to taste

2 tablespoons chopped fresh parsley leaves

½ teaspoon kosher salt

¼ teaspoon freshly ground black pepper

¼ teaspoon crushed red pepper flakes, optional

1 pound medium shrimp, unpeeled

Crusty bread brushed with olive oil, for serving

1. Preheat a gas or charcoal grill over high heat.

2. In a small bowl, whisk together the melted butter, garlic, lemon juice, parsley, salt, pepper, and red pepper flakes, if desired.

3. Tear off 4 sheets of foil, each about 12 inches long. Divide the shrimp into 4 equal portions, and arrange each portion in the center of a piece of foil in a single layer.

4. Fold up all 4 sides of each foil packet. Spoon the garlic butter mixture over the shrimp, dividing it evenly. Fold the sides of the foil over the shrimp, covering it completely and sealing the packets closed.

5. Grill the shrimp in the foil packets until the shrimp are just cooked through, 7 to 8 minutes (see Note). Serve immediately with crusty bread, if desired.

Note: Alternatively, bake the foil packets for 8 to 10 minutes in a preheated 425°F oven.

TIP
This shrimp packet is loaded with flavor, while managing to remain low in sodium and calories.

PER SERVING: CALORIES 180 FAT 12g PROTEIN 17g CARB 1g FIBER 0g CHOL 167mg IRON 1mg SODIUM 346mg CALC 66mg

This simple stir-fry recipe stars shrimp and broccoli, but the sauce will work with any veggie combination you might want to toss together. The only downside is that cooking the rice will take longer than making the actual recipe!

SHRIMP *and* BROCCOLI STIR-FRY

SERVES 4   PREP TIME: 10 MINUTES   TOTAL TIME: 20 MINUTES

FOR THE STIR-FRY SAUCE

3 tablespoons reduced-sodium soy sauce

2 tablespoons oyster sauce

1 tablespoon rice wine vinegar

1 tablespoon packed brown sugar

1 tablespoon freshly grated ginger

2 cloves garlic, minced

1 teaspoon sesame oil

1 teaspoon cornstarch

1 teaspoon Sriracha sauce, optional

2 tablespoons olive oil

12 ounces broccoli florets

1 ½ pounds medium shrimp, peeled and deveined

2 cups cooked white or brown rice

1 teaspoon sesame seeds, for garnish

1 green onion, thinly sliced, for garnish, optional

1. Make the stir-fry sauce: In a small bowl, whisk together the soy sauce, oyster sauce, vinegar, brown sugar, ginger, garlic, sesame oil, cornstarch, and Sriracha, if desired; set aside.

2. Heat 1 tablespoon of the olive oil in a large skillet over medium-high heat. Add the broccoli, and cook, stirring frequently, for 3 minutes. Toss the shrimp with the remaining 1 tablespoon oil, and add to the skillet; cook, stirring frequently, until the shrimp turn pink and the broccoli florets are tender, about 3 minutes.

3. Stir in the stir-fry sauce until well combined and slightly thickened, about 1 minute.

4. Serve the stir-fry immediately on top of the rice. Garnish with the sesame seeds and green onions, if desired.

PER SERVING: CALORIES 350 FAT 9.1g PROTEIN 31g CARB 36g FIBER 3g CHOL 205mg IRON 2mg SODIUM 901mg CALC 138mg

The secret to perfectly seared scallops requires you to remember just two things: (1) pat the scallops completely dry with paper towels, and (2) have a hot pan ready. That's it!

LEMON BUTTER SCALLOPS

SERVES 4   PREP TIME: 6 MINUTES   TOTAL TIME: 17 MINUTES   `GF`

1 pound scallops

Kosher salt and freshly ground black pepper, to taste

1 tablespoon unsalted butter

FOR THE LEMON BUTTER SAUCE

2 tablespoons unsalted butter

2 cloves garlic, minced

Juice of 1 lemon

Kosher salt and freshly ground black pepper, to taste

2 tablespoons chopped fresh parsley leaves, for garnish, optional

1. Remove the small side muscle from each scallop, and discard. Rinse the scallops with cold water, and thoroughly pat dry. Season the scallops with salt and pepper to taste.

2. Melt the butter in a large skillet over medium-high heat until very hot.

3. Working in batches, add the scallops to the skillet in a single layer, and cook, flipping once, until golden brown on the outside and translucent in the center, 1 to 2 minutes per side. Transfer to a plate, and keep warm.

4. Make the lemon butter sauce: Melt the butter in the same skillet over medium-high heat. Add the garlic, and cook, stirring frequently, until fragrant, about 1 minute. Stir in the lemon juice; season with salt and pepper to taste.

5. Serve the scallops immediately with the lemon butter sauce and garnished with parsley, if desired.

PER SERVING: CALORIES 159 FAT 9.2g PROTEIN 14g CARB 5g FIBER 0g CHOL 50mg IRON 1mg SODIUM 688mg CALC 14mg

I love how versatile this recipe is. You can serve it as an appetizer or as an entrée with a side of broccoli (page 177) or maybe potatoes. It is definitely a dish that is fancy enough for dinner guests. Plus, who can say no to bacon, garlic, and butter?

BACON-WRAPPED SCALLOPS
with GARLIC BUTTER SAUCE

SERVES 4   PREP TIME: 15 MINUTES   TOTAL TIME: 30 MINUTES   `GF`

1 pound large scallops

Freshly ground black pepper, to taste

6 ounces bacon

2 tablespoons olive oil

FOR THE GARLIC BUTTER SAUCE

½ cup unsalted butter

3 cloves garlic, minced

1 teaspoon dried Italian seasoning

½ teaspoon crushed red pepper flakes, optional

Kosher salt and freshly ground black pepper, to taste

2 tablespoons chopped fresh parsley leaves, for garnish, optional

1. Preheat the broiler. Lightly oil a baking sheet or coat with nonstick spray.

2. Remove the small side muscle from each scallop, and discard. Rinse the scallops with cold water and thoroughly pat dry. Season with pepper.

3. Wrap each scallop with bacon, securing with a toothpick.

4. Place the scallops on the prepared baking sheet, and drizzle with olive oil. Broil until the bacon is crisp and cooked through, turning once, 10 to 15 minutes (see Note).

5. Make the garlic butter sauce: Melt the butter in a large skillet over medium-high heat. Add the garlic, Italian seasoning, and red pepper flakes, if desired, and cook, stirring frequently, until fragrant, about 2 minutes. Season with salt and pepper to taste.

6. Serve scallops immediately with the garlic butter sauce and garnished with parsley, if desired.

Note: The scallops can also be grilled over medium-high heat until cooked through, 7 to 10 minutes.

PER SERVING: CALORIES 532 FAT 48.4g PROTEIN 20g CARB 5g FIBER 0g CHOL 116mg IRON 1mg SODIUM 850mg CALC 25mg

What's not to like about the luscious-firm goodness of broiled lobster tails dipped in a buttery parsley-lemon sauce that just melts in your mouth? This version requires minimal prep so it comes together at lightning speed. You can serve this indulgence for special date nights, anniversaries, or even as a weeknight treat—it's just that easy.

BROILED LOBSTER TAILS

SERVES 4   PREP TIME: 15 MINUTES   TOTAL TIME: 25 MINUTES   GF

½ cup unsalted butter, melted

2 tablespoons freshly squeezed lemon juice, or more to taste

2 tablespoons chopped fresh parsley leaves

3 cloves garlic, minced

½ teaspoon crushed red pepper flakes, optional

Kosher salt and freshly ground black pepper, to taste

4 fresh lobster tails

1. Preheat the broiler. Lightly oil a 9- x 9-inch baking dish, or coat it with nonstick spray.

2. In a small bowl, whisk together the melted butter, lemon juice, parsley, garlic, and red pepper flakes, if desired; season with salt and pepper to taste. Set aside.

3. Using sharp kitchen shears, carefully cut the top side of each lobster shell lengthwise, from the head to the base of the tail. Pull the shells apart slightly, and separate the meat from the shells.

4. Arrange the tails in the prepared baking dish in a single layer; brush with the butter mixture, reserving 2 tablespoons.

5. Broil until the lobster tails are lightly browned and the flesh is opaque, 5 to 8 minutes.

6. Serve immediately with the reserved butter mixture.

PER SERVING: CALORIES 302 FAT 25g PROTEIN 18g CARB 1g FIBER 0g CHOL 196mg IRON 0mg SODIUM 574mg CALC 103mg

I never go
to a potluck
without these.

These are addictive. Bet
you can't stop at one.

7

APPETIZERS & SIDES IN A SNAP

From creamy, cheesy dips that please a crowd to essential (and foolproof) sides, these are super-simple, super-fast recipes that will see you through any type of entertaining. Don't be surprised when people start coming back for more and more.

I love these garlic knots. They're so quick to prepare—all you need is 10 spare minutes. The secret is using refrigerated biscuit dough, and, of course, freshly grated Parmesan is always best!

EASY GARLIC PARMESAN KNOTS

MAKES 16 KNOTS   **PREP TIME:** 10 MINUTES   **TOTAL TIME:** 22 MINUTES   KF

¼ cup unsalted butter, melted

2 tablespoons freshly grated Parmesan cheese

¾ teaspoon garlic powder

½ teaspoon dried oregano

½ teaspoon dried parsley

¼ teaspoon salt

1 (16.3-ounce) tube refrigerated buttermilk biscuits

1. Preheat the oven to 400°F. Lightly oil a baking sheet, or coat with nonstick spray.

2. In a small bowl, whisk together the melted butter, Parmesan, garlic powder, oregano, parsley, and salt; set aside.

3. Halve each of the 8 biscuits to make 16 pieces of dough. Roll each piece into a 5-inch-long rope, about ½ inch thick, and tie each rope into a knot, tucking in the ends to seal.

4. Put the knots on the prepared baking sheet, spacing them out evenly, and brush the tops of the knots with half the butter mixture. Bake until golden brown, 10 to 12 minutes.

5. Serve immediately, brushed with the remaining butter mixture.

PER SERVING: CALORIES 99 **FAT** 4.1g **PROTEIN** 2g **CARB** 14g **FIBER** 0g **CHOL** 8mg **IRON** 1mg **SODIUM** 289mg **CALC** 14mg

Remember when you hated any type of green veggie, most notably broccoli, as a child? Well, if Mom had ever dressed it up with garlic and Parmesan, we wouldn't have had a problem. This is just one of those universally popular side dishes that goes well with almost everything.

GARLIC-PARMESAN ROASTED BROCCOLI

SERVES 6   PREP TIME: 5 MINUTES   TOTAL TIME: 23 MINUTES   GF   KF

2 (12-ounce) packages broccoli florets (about 10 cups)

3 tablespoons olive oil

4 cloves garlic, minced

Kosher salt and freshly ground black pepper, to taste

¼ cup freshly grated Parmesan cheese

Juice of 1 lemon

TIP

The fat from the Parmesan will actually help your body absorb the fat-soluble vitamins—A, E, and K— found in the broccoli.

1. Preheat the oven to 425°F. Lightly oil a baking sheet, or coat it with nonstick spray.

2. Put the broccoli florets on the prepared baking sheet. Sprinkle with the olive oil and garlic, and gently toss to combine. Season with salt and pepper to taste, and then spread the florets out in a single layer.

3. Roast the broccoli for 12 to 18 minutes, or until tender and lightly browned.

4. Serve immediately, sprinkled with the Parmesan and lemon juice.

PER SERVING: CALORIES 136 FAT 10g PROTEIN 5g CARB 9g FIBER 3g CHOL 3mg IRON 1mg SODIUM 282mg CALC 124mg

Prepped in just 5 minutes, this veggie dip is irresistibly tangy and creamy—and perfect for snacking. Serve with fresh veggies, whole-grain crackers, or baked chips for smarter nibbling. We can keep the lightened-with-Greek-yogurt situation between you and me.

RANCH VEGGIE DIP

SERVES 6   **PREP TIME:** 5 MINUTES   **TOTAL TIME:** 5 MINUTES PLUS CHILLING   `GF` `KF` `VEG`

½ cup sour cream

½ cup plain Greek yogurt

¼ cup mayonnaise (see Note)

1 tablespoon freshly squeezed lemon juice

1 teaspoon dried parsley

½ teaspoon dried basil

½ teaspoon dried dill

¼ teaspoon garlic powder

¼ teaspoon onion powder

½ teaspoon kosher salt

¼ teaspoon freshly ground black pepper

2 tablespoons chopped fresh parsley leaves, for garnish, optional

Assorted vegetables

1. In a large bowl, whisk together the sour cream, yogurt, mayonnaise, lemon juice, parsley, basil, dill, garlic powder, and onion powder; season with salt and pepper.

2. Refrigerate, covered, for at least 1 hour.

3. Garnish with parsley, if desired, and serve with vegetables for dipping.

Note: Additional Greek yogurt can be sustituted for the mayonnaise, if desired.

PER SERVING: CALORIES 121 **FAT** 11g **PROTEIN** 3g **CARB** 2g **FIBER** 0g **CHOL** 20mg **IRON** 0mg **SODIUM** 233mg **CALC** 40mg

This is a must-make dip for any party. Serve it in a baking dish with toasted baguette, tortilla chips, or pita for dipping, or in a bread bowl with spoons for your more ambitious guests. Don't judge them; this creamy pool of cheesy, chunky goodness is just that good.

CHUNKY ARTICHOKE, SPINACH, *and* JALAPEÑO DIP

SERVES 8   PREP TIME: 10 MINUTES   TOTAL TIME: 30 MINUTES

1 (8-ounce) package cream cheese, at room temperature

¼ cup mayonnaise

¼ cup sour cream

¼ teaspoon garlic powder

¼ teaspoon onion powder

1 (14-ounce) can artichoke hearts, drained and chopped

1 (4-ounce) can diced jalapeño chiles

3 cups loosely packed baby spinach, chopped

1 cup shredded mozzarella cheese

¼ cup crumbled feta or goat cheese

¼ cup freshly grated Parmesan cheese

Kosher salt and freshly ground black pepper, to taste

2 tablespoons chopped fresh chives, for garnish, optional

1. Preheat the oven to 375°F. Lightly oil a 9-inch baking dish, or coat it with nonstick spray.

2. In a large bowl, mix together the cream cheese, mayonnaise, sour cream, garlic powder, and onion powder. Stir in the artichoke hearts, jalapeños, spinach, ½ cup of the mozzarella, the feta, and Parmesan; season with salt and pepper to taste.

3. Evenly spread the cream cheese mixture into the prepared baking dish; sprinkle with the remaining ½ cup mozzarella.

4. Bake until the dip is bubbly and golden, 15 to 20 minutes.

5. Serve immediately, garnished with the chives, if desired.

PER SERVING: CALORIES 258 FAT 20.2g PROTEIN 9g CARB 6g FIBER 2g CHOL 52mg IRON 1mg SODIUM 556mg CALC 234mg

Once you eat one of these, it's game over. They are so addictive that I may have finished off all four servings by myself. In a span of 5 minutes. Maybe it was less, but who's counting? Don't bother trying to resist them.

ZUCCHINI PARMESAN CRISPS

SERVES 4 **PREP TIME:** 15 MINUTES **TOTAL TIME:** 25 MINUTES KF

½ cup vegetable oil

½ cup all-purpose flour

2 large eggs, beaten

Kosher salt and freshly ground black pepper

1 cup panko

½ cup grated Parmesan cheese

2 zucchini, thinly sliced into ¼-inch-thick rounds

Kosher salt

2 tablespoons chopped fresh chives for garnish, optional

1. Heat the vegetable oil in a large nonstick skillet over medium-high heat.

2. Put the flour in a shallow bowl. Pour the beaten eggs into another shallow bowl, season with salt and pepper, and whisk to blend. In a large bowl, toss together the panko and Parmesan to evenly distribute.

3. Working in batches, dredge the zucchini slices in the flour, dip into the eggs, and then dredge in the panko mixture, pressing to coat.

4. Add the zucchini slices to the skillet, five or six at a time, and cook until evenly golden and crispy, about 1 minute per side. Transfer to a paper towel–lined plate to drain.

5. Sprinkle with salt while still hot from the skillet. Serve immediately garnished with the chives, if desired.

PER SERVING: CALORIES 314 **FAT** 17.3g **PROTEIN** 14g **CARB** 27g **FIBER** 2g **CHOL** 103mg **IRON** 1mg **SODIUM** 442mg **CALC** 232mg

Everyone loves these fritters. Use them to sneak veggies onto your picky eater's plate as an appetizer, side dish, or after-school snack. You can easily double (or triple) the recipe and freeze the leftovers to use as needed so you can always get your zucchini fix.

ZUCCHINI FRITTERS

SERVES 4   PREP TIME: 10 MINUTES   TOTAL TIME: 25 MINUTES   KF   VEG

1 ½ pounds zucchini, grated (see Note)

1 teaspoon kosher salt

¼ cup all-purpose flour

¼ cup freshly grated Parmesan cheese

2 cloves garlic, minced

1 large egg, beaten

Kosher salt and freshly ground black pepper, to taste

¼ cup olive oil

TIP

These can be frozen in a zip-top plastic freezer bag and reheated in the oven at 350°F for 8 to 10 minutes.

1. Place the grated zucchini in a colander over the sink. Add the salt, and gently toss to combine; let sit for 5 minutes. Using a clean dish towel or cheesecloth, drain the zucchini completely, removing as much water as possible.

2. In a large bowl, combine the drained zucchini, flour, Parmesan, garlic, and egg; season with salt and pepper to taste.

3. Heat olive oil in a large skillet over medium-high heat. Scoop 2 tablespoons of batter for each fritter, flattening with a spatula, and cook until the underside is golden brown, about 2 minutes. Flip over, and cook on the other side, 1 to 2 minutes longer. Serve immediately.

Note: 1 ½ pounds zucchini (4 to 5 medium zucchini) = 3 cups grated

PER SERVING: CALORIES 167 **FAT** 10.6g **PROTEIN** 8g **CARB** 12g **FIBER** 2g **CHOL** 52mg **IRON** 1mg **SODIUM** 637mg **CALC** 139mg

Amazingly crisp on the outside and tender on the inside, these zucchini-and-carrot-loaded tots are both kid- and adult-friendly. And after trying these, you (and the kids) may never want to go back to the traditional potato tots again. Hey, you save on calories and you get veggies packed right in. That's a win-win right there.

ZUCCHINI TOTS

SERVES 6   PREP TIME: 15 MINUTES   TOTAL TIME: 30 MINUTES   **KF**

2 zucchini, grated

½ teaspoon kosher salt

2 carrots, peeled and shredded

½ cup panko

2 large eggs, beaten

¼ cup shredded Cheddar cheese

2 tablespoons freshly grated
   Parmesan cheese

½ teaspoon dried basil

½ teaspoon dried oregano

¼ teaspoon garlic powder

¼ teaspoon onion powder

Pinch of Cajun seasoning, optional

Kosher salt and freshly ground black
   pepper, to taste

2 tablespoons chopped fresh parsley
   leaves, for garnish, optional

1. Preheat the oven to 400°F. Lightly oil a baking sheet, or coat it with nonstick spray.

2. Put the grated zucchini in a colander over the sink. Add the salt and gently toss to combine; let sit for 5 minutes. Using a clean dish towel or cheesecloth, drain the zucchini completely, removing as much water as possible.

3. Transfer the drained zucchini to a large bowl. Stir in the shredded carrots, panko, beaten eggs, both cheeses, the basil, oregano, garlic powder, onion powder, and Cajun seasoning, if desired; season with salt and pepper to taste.

4. Form the zucchini-and-carrot mixture into approximately 2-inch-long tots, and arrange them on the prepared baking sheet, leaving space between them.

5. Bake until golden brown and crisp, 15 to 16 minutes, flipping before the last 10 minutes of cooking time.

6. Serve immediately, garnished with the parsley, if desired.

Note: Zucchini tots can be frozen and reheated later. Transfer the cooled tots to an airtight container and freeze for up to 1 month. To reheat, bake at 400°F until heated through, 15 to 16 minutes.

PER SERVING: **CALORIES** 104 **FAT** 4.5g **PROTEIN** 6g **CARB** 10g **FIBER** 2g **CHOL** 68mg **IRON** 1mg **SODIUM** 285mg **CALC** 96mg

The creamy notes of the mushroom stock soak into the wholesome brown rice. Just add tofu or chicken, such as my All-Purpose Chicken (page 145) to make this side dish a complete meal.

MUSHROOM RICE

SERVES 6   PREP TIME: 10 MINUTES   TOTAL TIME: 40 MINUTES   VEG

1 tablespoon olive oil

2 cloves garlic, minced

1 onion, diced

1 pound cremini mushrooms, thinly sliced

2 teaspoons Worcestershire sauce

1/2 teaspoon dried thyme

Kosher salt and freshly ground black pepper, to taste

3/4 cup uncooked white or brown rice

1 1/2 cups vegetable broth

2 tablespoons unsalted butter

2 tablespoons chopped fresh chives, for garnish, optional

1. Heat the olive oil in a large stockpot or Dutch oven over medium heat. Add the garlic and onion, and cook, stirring frequently, about 2 to 3 minutes, until the onion is translucent.

2. Stir in the mushrooms, Worcestershire, and thyme, and cook, stirring occasionally, until the mushrooms are tender and browned, 5 to 6 minutes; season with salt and pepper to taste.

3. Stir in the white rice and vegetable broth. Bring to a boil; cover, reduce the heat, and simmer until the rice is cooked through and the broth has been absorbed, 20 to 25 minutes. (If using brown rice, cooking time will increase to 40 to 45 minutes.) Stir in the butter until melted, about 1 minute.

4. Serve immediately, garnished with the chives, if desired.

PER SERVING: CALORIES 171 FAT 6.8g PROTEIN 4g CARB 25g FIBER 2g CHOL 10mg IRON 1mg SODIUM 342mg CALC 33mg

TIP

Although its cooking time is longer, brown rice is more nutritious than white rice, with more flavor, iron, and magnesium.

When you have a hankering for greasy fast-food french fries, these asparagus "fries" will satisfy that craving. Baked to absolute crisp perfection, they're quick to whip up and so much healthier. Serve them with the Ranch Veggie Dip (page 178).

BAKED ASPARAGUS FRIES

SERVES 4   PREP TIME: 15 MINUTES   TOTAL TIME: 27 MINUTES   KF

1 cup panko

½ cup freshly grated Parmesan cheese

Kosher salt and freshly ground black pepper, to taste

1 pound asparagus, trimmed

½ cup all-purpose flour

2 large eggs, beaten

1. Preheat the oven to 425°F. Lightly oil a baking sheet, or coat it with nonstick spray.

2. In a large bowl, combine the panko and Parmesan; season with salt and pepper to taste. Set aside.

3. Working in batches, dredge the asparagus spears in the flour, dip into the eggs, and then dredge in the panko mixture, pressing to coat.

4. Arrange the asparagus in a single layer on the prepared baking sheet. Bake for 10 to 12 minutes, or until golden brown and crisp. Serve immediately.

PER SERVING: CALORIES 206 FAT 2.4g PROTEIN 12g CARB 25g FIBER 3g CHOL 93mg IRON 0mg SODIUM 36mg CALC 14mg

Finally, a cheesy dip you can enjoy guilt free, made "skinny" with Greek yogurt instead of more mayonnaise. No one will be able to tell the difference. The dip is great during tailgating season since you can prep everything beforehand. Just pop it in the oven right before you are ready to serve.

HOT *and* CHEESY CORN DIP

SERVES 8   PREP TIME: 10 MINUTES   TOTAL TIME: 25 MINUTES   `KF` `VEG`

3 cups corn kernels, frozen (thawed), canned, or roasted

1 (4.5-ounce) can chopped green chiles, drained

1½ cups shredded mozzarella cheese

1 cup plain Greek yogurt

¼ cup mayonnaise (see Note)

2 tablespoons chopped fresh cilantro leaves, plus more for garnish, optional

½ teaspoon garlic powder

½ teaspoon onion powder

½ teaspoon dried oregano

1 teaspoon kosher salt

½ teaspoon freshly ground black pepper

1 Roma tomato, diced

2 green onions, thinly sliced

1. Preheat the oven to 400°F. Lightly oil a 9-inch baking dish, or coat it with nonstick spray.

2. In a large bowl, stir together the corn, chiles, 1 cup of the mozzarella, the yogurt, mayonnaise, cilantro, garlic powder, onion powder, and oregano until well combined; season with salt and pepper.

3. Spread the corn mixture into the prepared baking dish; sprinkle the top with the remaining ½ cup mozzarella.

4. Bake until bubbly around the edges, about 15 minutes.

5. Serve immediately, garnished with the tomato, green onions, and additional cilantro, if desired.

Note: Additional Greek yogurt can be sustituted for the mayonnaise, if desired.

PER SERVING: CALORIES 170 FAT 9.5g PROTEIN 7g CARB 15g FIBER 1g CHOL 12mg IRON 0mg SODIUM 425mg CALC 124mg

This is one of my favorite tapas to whip up when I'm in a rush. They require minimal prep and zero cooking! Simply thread your tomatoes, salami, and mozzarella, and then drizzle with garlic basil oil. That's it! (The basil oil can also be made ahead of time.) These are the perfect accompaniment to the Spaghetti Carbonara (page 140).

CAPRESE BITES *with* GARLIC BASIL OIL

SERVES 4   PREP TIME: 5 MINUTES   TOTAL TIME: 5 MINUTES

FOR THE GARLIC BASIL OIL

¼ cup olive oil

1 teaspoon balsamic vinegar

¼ cup fresh basil leaves, finely chopped

2 cloves garlic, pressed

Kosher salt and freshly ground black pepper, to taste

12 cherry tomatoes

12 slices salami or pepperoni

12 ovoline fresh mozzarella, halved

1. Make the garlic basil oil: In a small bowl, whisk together the olive oil, balsamic vinegar, basil, and garlic; season with salt and pepper to taste. Set aside.

2. Thread tomatoes, salami, and mozzarella onto 4-inch-long skewers or toothpicks.

3. Serve immediately, drizzled with garlic basil oil.

PER SERVING: CALORIES 235 **FAT** 21.8g **PROTEIN** 8g **CARB** 3g **FIBER** 1g **CHOL** 30mg **IRON** 1mg **SODIUM** 331mg **CALC** 13mg

These Korean-style pancakes are quick, easy, and perfectly spicy. For a clean-out-the-fridge appetizer, you can throw in more veggies, if you like! Plus, the drizzled cream sauce is absolutely everything.

KOREAN KIMCHI PANCAKES

SERVES 4   PREP TIME: 15 MINUTES   TOTAL TIME: 25 MINUTES   VEG

FOR THE SRIRACHA CREAM SAUCE

¼ cup mayonnaise

1 tablespoon Sriracha sauce

1 tablespoon sweetened condensed milk

1 cup all-purpose flour

1 cup kimchi, drained and chopped, juices reserved (see Note)

1 zucchini, grated

2 green onions, chopped

½ teaspoon salt

½ teaspoon sugar

1 tablespoon vegetable oil

1. Make the Sriracha cream sauce: In a small bowl, whisk together the mayonnaise, Sriracha, and condensed milk; set aside.

2. In a large bowl, stir together the flour, kimchi, zucchini, green onions, salt, and sugar until well combined.

3. Heat the oil in a large skillet over medium-high heat. When the oil is very hot, scoop about ¼ cup of batter for each pancake, flatten each one with a spatula, and cook until the undersides are nicely golden brown, about 2 minutes. Flip and cook on the other side, 1 to 2 minutes longer.

4. Serve immediately, drizzled with the Sriracha cream sauce.

Note: Kimchi is now available in the produce aisle of many grocery stores.

PER SERVING: CALORIES 284 FAT 14.7g PROTEIN 4g CARB 34g FIBER 2g CHOL 7mg IRON 2mg SODIUM 800mg CALC 53mg

TIP

These can be frozen in a zip-top plastic freezer bag and reheated in the oven at 350°F for 8 to 10 minutes (sans cream sauce of course).

Say good-bye to fast-food chicken nuggets and hello to amazingly crispy, tender homemade chicken goodness. The secret here is using peanut oil which yields a pleasing nutty flavor.

PARMESAN CHICKEN BITES

SERVES 4   PREP TIME: 15 MINUTES   TOTAL TIME: 25 MINUTES   KF

½ cup peanut oil

1 pound boneless, skinless chicken breasts, cut into 1-inch chunks

¾ teaspoon kosher salt

½ teaspoon freshly ground black pepper

1 cup panko

¼ cup freshly grated Parmesan cheese, plus more for serving

1 teaspoon garlic powder

½ teaspoon smoked paprika

Kosher salt and freshly ground black pepper, to taste

½ cup all-purpose flour

2 large eggs, beaten

2 tablespoons chopped fresh parsley leaves, for garnish, optional

1. Heat the oil in a large skillet over medium heat.

2. Season the chicken pieces with the salt and pepper.

3. In a large bowl, combine the panko, Parmesan, garlic powder, and smoked paprika; season with salt and pepper to taste. Put the flour and the beaten eggs in separate shallow bowls.

4. Working in batches, dredge the chicken in the flour, dip into the eggs, and then dredge in the panko mixture, pressing to coat.

5. Add the chicken to the skillet, 5 or 6 at a time, and cook until evenly golden and crispy, 3 to 4 minutes. Transfer to a paper towel–lined plate to drain.

6. Serve immediately, sprinkled with additional Parmesan and garnished with the parsley, if desired.

PER SERVING: CALORIES 400 FAT 19.5g PROTEIN 35g CARB 20g FIBER 1g CHOL 163mg IRON 2mg SODIUM 625mg CALC 120mg

TIP

Peanut oil is heat-stable and contains mainly healthy monounsaturated fatty acids.

These little morsels are surefire crowd-pleasers. I mean, we're talking bacon and mini sausages. They're great for parties or on game days since they are easy to assemble beforehand. Secure using fancy toothpicks to dress them up.

BACON-WRAPPED SMOKIES

SERVES 8 **PREP TIME:** 15 MINUTES **TOTAL TIME:** 45 MINUTES **KF**

1 (16-ounce) package beef cocktail sausages, drained and rinsed

8 slices bacon, cut crosswise into quarters

¼ cup packed light brown sugar

Freshly ground black pepper

1 tablespoon chopped fresh parsley leaves, for garnish, optional

1. Preheat the oven to 350°F. Line a baking sheet with parchment paper or a silicone baking mat; set aside.

2. Working one at a time, wrap each sausage in a piece of bacon, and dredge in the brown sugar, pressing to coat.

3. Carefully place the wrapped sausages, seam sides down, on the prepared baking sheet. Bake until the brown sugar has caramelized and the bacon is crisp, 25 to 30 minutes.

4. Serve immediately, seasoned with pepper and garnished with the parsley, if desired.

PER SERVING: CALORIES 218 **FAT** 15.4g **PROTEIN** 8g **CARB** 9g **FIBER** 1g **CHOL** 38mg **IRON** 1mg **SODIUM** 720mg **CALC** 18mg

You can make this teriyaki sauce completely from scratch with just a few pantry ingredients and let your shrimp skewers marinate overnight. When you're ready to serve, throw the skewers on the grill and have them on the table in less than 10 minutes for the quickest teriyaki fix in town. Drizzle with the Sriracha Cream Sauce (page 196)—didn't I tell you it would come in handy?

TERIYAKI-SRIRACHA SHRIMP SKEWERS

SERVES 4   PREP TIME: 20 MINUTES   TOTAL TIME: 30 MINUTES PLUS MARINATING

FOR THE TERIYAKI MARINADE

1/4 cup reduced-sodium soy sauce

1/4 cup packed brown sugar

3 cloves garlic, minced

1 tablespoon honey

1 tablespoon freshly grated ginger

1 cup water

1 tablespoon cornstarch

1/4 cup water

1 1/2 pounds medium shrimp, peeled and deveined

2 tablespoons chopped fresh cilantro leaves, for garnish

1 teaspoon sesame seeds, for garnish

1 recipe Sriracha cream sauce (page 196)

1. Make the teriyaki marinade: In a small saucepan over medium heat, whisk together the soy sauce, brown sugar, garlic, honey, ginger, and 1 cup water; bring to a simmer, whisking until the brown sugar has dissolved.

2. In a small bowl, whisk together the cornstarch and 1/4 cup water. Stir the cornstarch mixture into the saucepan until the teriyaki marinade has thickened enough to coat the back of a spoon, about 2 minutes; let cool to room temperature.

3. Thread the shrimp onto 4 metal skewers. In a gallon-sized zip-top bag or large bowl, combine the teriyaki marinade and the shrimp skewers; marinate for at least 30 minutes or up to overnight, turning the bag occasionally.

4. Preheat a gas or charcoal grill, or place a grill pan over medium-high heat. Add the shrimp skewers to the grill, and cook just until the shrimp are pink, firm, and cooked through, 2 to 3 minutes per side.

5. Garnish the shrimp with the cilantro and sesame seeds, and serve immediately with the Sriracha cream sauce.

PER SERVING: CALORIES 320 FAT 11.7g PROTEIN 27g CARB 26g FIBER 0g CHOL 213mg IRON 1mg SODIUM 862mg CALC 114mg

These five-ingredient mini pizzas are unbelievably easy and foolproof, too. Baking the pizzas in a muffin tin delivers just the right deep-dish crispness. Feel free to play around with the recipe, adding different pizza toppings to suit your guests' preferences. Although you could never go wrong with the classic pepperoni topping.

MINI DEEP-DISH PIZZAS

MAKES 12 MINI PIZZAS   **PREP TIME:** 15 MINUTES   **TOTAL TIME:** 25 MINUTES   `KF`

4 (8-inch) flour tortillas

1 cup pizza sauce

³/₄ cup shredded mozzarella cheese

¹/₄ cup freshly grated Parmesan cheese

36 to 48 slices mini pepperoni

2 tablespoons chopped fresh parsley leaves, for garnish, optional

1. Preheat the oven to 425°F. Lightly oil a 12-cup muffin tin, or coat it with nonstick spray.

2. Working one at a time, lay a tortilla on a flat surface. Using an empty 14 ¹/₂-ounce can, cut out 3 rounds from the tortilla, pressing firmly and using a rocking motion to cut all the way through the tortilla. Repeat with the remaining tortillas.

3. Press a tortilla round into each of the 12 prepared muffin cups, pressing down carefully to create a well in the center of each cup. Scoop 1 tablespoon pizza sauce into each muffin tin. Sprinkle with the mozzarella and Parmesan, dividing it evenly, and top each pizza with 3 to 5 slices of mini pepperoni.

4. Bake for 10 to 12 minutes, or until both cheeses have melted.

5. Serve immediately, garnished with the parsley, if desired.

PER SERVING: CALORIES 104 **FAT** 4.5g **PROTEIN** 5g **CARB** 10g **FIBER** 1g **CHOL** 8mg **IRON** 0mg **SODIUM** 369mg **CALC** 84mg

My spin on a Girl
Scout classic.

This is a
6-minute dessert!

8

LAST-MINUTE DRINKS & DESSERTS

Confession Time: Even though I love eating them, I'm not really known for baking desserts, so I rely on easy-peasy sweets that anyone can master. Here are sips and bites that are irresistible but simple to make—because who can wait before getting to all the awesomeness?

I have been making a daily stop at my local coffee shop for their mint mojito iced coffee ever since I moved back to Los Angeles 3 years ago. It may just be the best cup of coffee I've ever had, but $4 per cup can start to add up! Fortunately for my wallet, I've figured out how to make a version at home with just a few ingredients. You can use your favorite kind of coffee, adding in more or less sugar to suit your taste preference. Easy and cheap enough, right?

MINT MOJITO ICED COFFEE

SERVES 1   PREP TIME: 5 MINUTES   TOTAL TIME: 5 MINUTES   GF   VEG

1 tablespoon turbinado sugar, plus more to taste

¼ cup loosely packed fresh mint leaves

1 cup hot coffee

2 tablespoons heavy cream

1 sprig fresh mint, for garnish, optional

1. Using the back of a spoon, pound the sugar and mint leaves together in a 12-ounce glass until fragrant, 1 to 2 minutes.

2. Stir in the hot coffee until the sugar has dissolved.

3. Serve immediately over ice, topped with the heavy cream and garnished with a mint sprig, if desired.

PER SERVING: CALORIES 165 **FAT** 11.2g **PROTEIN** 1g **CARB** 16g **FIBER** 1g **CHOL** 41mg **IRON** 0mg **SODIUM** 19mg **CALC** 41mg

Skip the store-bought cocoa mix: Homemade hot chocolate is easier to make than you think with just a handful of ingredients that are already sitting in your pantry. And this adult version—with a hint of Kahlúa—is an extra-special treat, especially during the holiday season.

KAHLÚA HOT CHOCOLATE

SERVES 2 **PREP TIME:** 5 MINUTES **TOTAL TIME:** 8 MINUTES `GF`

2 cups whole milk

2 tablespoons sugar

1 1/2 tablespoons Dutch-process unsweetened cocoa powder

1/4 teaspoon ground cinnamon

Pinch of nutmeg

1 ounce Kahlúa coffee liqueur

OPTIONAL TOPPINGS

Mini marshmallows

Salted caramel

Chocolate syrup

1. In a medium saucepan, combine the milk, sugar, cocoa powder, cinnamon, and nutmeg over medium heat; stir until the milk is heated through and the sugar has dissolved, 2 to 3 minutes. Remove from the heat, and stir in the Kahlúa.

2. Serve immediately, garnished with mini marshmallows, salted caramel, and/or chocolate syrup, if desired.

PER SERVING: CALORIES 263 **FAT** 8.5g **PROTEIN** 9g **CARB** 34g **FIBER** 1g **CHOL** 30mg **IRON** 1mg **SODIUM** 121mg **CALC** 304mg

Wonderfully refreshing, bubbly, and sweet, you can make this exceptional cocktail in minutes to impress the guests at your next party. Swap out the raspberries for strawberries, blueberries, blackberries—or a combination of all three! Just be sure to let the berries freeze for at least 30 minutes so they will keep your drink chilled.

RASPBERRY LIMONCELLO PROSECCO

SERVES 8   PREP TIME: 5 MINUTES   TOTAL TIME: 5 MINUTES   GF VEG

1 (750-mL) bottle Prosecco, chilled

1 cup limoncello liqueur, chilled

2 cups frozen raspberries

8 sprigs fresh mint, for garnish, optional

1. In a large pitcher, whisk together the Prosecco and limoncello.

2. Serve over the raspberries, garnished with mint sprigs, if desired.

PER SERVING: CALORIES 181 FAT 0g PROTEIN 0g CARB 19g FIBER 2g CHOL 0mg IRON 0mg SODIUM 2mg CALC 9mg

The freshly squeezed grapefruit juice adds a fun splash of color to these easy mimosas.

GRAPEFRUIT MIMOSAS

SERVES 8   PREP TIME: 5 MINUTES   TOTAL TIME: 5 MINUTES   GF VEG

4 large ruby red grapefruits, juiced (about 3 cups)

1 (25.4-ounce) bottle sparkling white wine, chilled

½ cup fresh raspberries, for garnish, optional

8 sprigs fresh mint, for garnish, optional

1. Pour the grapefruit juice into champagne flutes until half full. Top off the glasses with the white wine.

2. Garnish with the raspberries, and serve immediately, with mint sprigs, if desired.

PER SERVING: CALORIES 123 FAT 0.4g PROTEIN 1g CARB 11g FIBER 1g CHOL 0mg IRON 0mg SODIUM 13mg CALC 10mg

Enjoy this refresher all summer long. Feel free to play around with the recipe, swapping out the strawberries for raspberries, blackberries, or even chunks of mango for a tropical twist. Whatever fruit flavors you choose, you can't go wrong with a frozen margarita!

STRAWBERRY-PINEAPPLE MARGARITA SLUSHIES

SERVES 4   PREP TIME: 5 MINUTES   TOTAL TIME: 5 MINUTES   GF   VEG

2 cups frozen strawberries

1 cup frozen pineapple chunks

2 ounces tequila

2 tablespoons triple sec

2 tablespoons sugar, optional

Juice of 1 lime

Coarse salt, for garnish, optional

1. In a blender, combine the strawberries, pineapple, tequila, triple sec, sugar, if using, and the lime juice with 2 cups ice, and puree until smooth.

2. Serve immediately. Garnish the rims of serving glasses with salt, if desired.

PER SERVING: CALORIES 96 FAT 0g PROTEIN 1g CARB 14g FIBER 1g CHOL 0mg IRON 0mg SODIUM 2mg CALC 18mg

TIP

Store-bought margarita mixes are nothing more than sugar and food coloring. They don't hold a candle to the real fruit in this recipe.

This is a quick summer treat—all you need is a blender, three ingredients, and five minutes. For a grown-up version, you can add a splash a vodka.

WATERMELON SLUSHIES

SERVES 4   **PREP TIME:** 5 MINUTES   **TOTAL TIME:** 5 MINUTES   GF   KF   VEG

5 cups diced seedless watermelon

2 tablespoons sugar

Juice of 1 lime

1. In a blender, combine the watermelon, sugar, lime juice, and 1 cup ice, and puree until smooth.

2. Serve immediately.

PER SERVING: CALORIES 74 **FAT** 0g **PROTEIN** 1g **CARB** 19g **FIBER** 1g **CHOL** 0mg **IRON** 0mg **SODIUM** 0mg **CALC** 13mg

TIP

Watermelons are more than 90% water, perfect for hydration on a hot day. They're also a great source of vitamin A and vitamin C.

Homemade fro-yo is easy to make, seriously refreshing, and best of all, totally guilt free. If you don't have strawberries on hand, swap in other fruit such as pineapple or cherries. For an adult version, add a tablespoon of rum to the mix.

STRAWBERRY BANANA FROZEN YOGURT

SERVES 4   PREP TIME: 10 MINUTES   TOTAL TIME: 10 MINUTES   `GF` `KF` `VEG`

1 pound strawberries, hulled and chopped

2 bananas

1 cup plain whole-milk yogurt (see Note)

½ cup sour cream

½ cup sugar

1 tablespoon freshly squeezed lemon juice

¼ teaspoon vanilla extract, optional

1. In a blender, combine the strawberries, bananas, yogurt, sour cream, sugar, lemon juice, and vanilla, if desired, and puree until smooth.

2. Pour the mixture into the bowl of an ice cream machine, and freeze according to manufacturer's instructions, about 25 minutes. Transfer to a freezer-safe container, and freeze until ready to serve.

Note: While fat-free yogurt can be substituted, whole-milk yogurt will yield a richer and smoother texture. Greek yogurt can also be substituted for the whole-milk yogurt.

PER SERVING: CALORIES 279 FAT 7.5g PROTEIN 4g CARB 50g FIBER 3g CHOL 28mg IRON 1mg SODIUM 41mg CALC 113mg

TIP

If you don't have an ice cream machine, don't worry. Start with frozen fruits, and then transfer everything to a freezer-safe container and freeze for a few hours.

A hint of spiciness along with the sweet make these candied nuts oh-so addictive. These are also perfect for a budget-friendly edible gift. Fill a jar and wrap a cute ribbon around it—your friends will thank you.

SPICY CINNAMON SUGAR CANDIED NUTS

MAKES 3 CUPS **PREP TIME:** 10 MINUTES **TOTAL TIME:** 35 MINUTES GF KF VEG

1 large egg white

2 teaspoons Sriracha sauce

1 tablespoon water

$\frac{1}{2}$ cup extra fine granulated sugar

$\frac{1}{4}$ cup packed light brown sugar

1 $\frac{1}{2}$ teaspoons cinnamon

1 cup raw almonds

1 cup raw pecans

1 cup raw walnuts

1. Preheat the oven to 300°F. Line a baking sheet with parchment paper; set aside.

2. In a small bowl, whisk together the egg white, Sriracha, and 1 tablespoon water until frothy, about 2 minutes; set aside.

3. In a medium bowl, combine the sugars and cinnamon; set aside.

4. In a large bowl, combine the almonds, pecans, walnuts, and the Sriracha mixture until well combined. Stir in the sugar mixture until evenly coated.

5. Spread the coated nuts evenly onto the prepared baking sheet. Bake for 20 to 25 minutes, stirring once.

6. Let cool completely before serving.

PER SERVING: CALORIES 240 **FAT** 18.7g **PROTEIN** 5g **CARB** 15g **FIBER** 3g **CHOL** 0mg **IRON** 1mg **SODIUM** 19mg **CALC** 47mg

Now you can indulge in a single-serving cookie made in just 6 minutes—5 minutes of prep time (or less) and 60 seconds in the microwave. For a special treat, top off this cookie-in-a-mug with ice cream and a drizzle of hot fudge. You can make many different variations by adding white chocolate chips or a mix of almonds, pecans, or even macadamia nuts. Feel free to experiment!

6-MINUTE CHOCOLATE-CHIP OATMEAL COOKIE

SERVES 1   PREP TIME: 5 MINUTES   TOTAL TIME: 6 MINUTES   KF   VEG

2 tablespoons unsalted butter, melted

2 tablespoons packed brown sugar

1 large egg yolk

1 tablespoon whole milk

¼ teaspoon vanilla extract

3 tablespoons all-purpose flour

1 tablespoon quick-cooking oats

¼ teaspoon baking powder

Pinch of nutmeg, optional

Pinch of salt

2 tablespoons semi-sweet chocolate chips

1. In a 12-ounce mug or bowl, whisk together the butter, brown sugar, egg yolk, milk, and vanilla. Whisk in the flour, oats, baking powder, nutmeg, if desired, and the salt until well combined. Stir in the chocolate chips.

2. Put the mug in the microwave, and cook for 60 seconds on high or until the cookie has puffed up and a toothpick inserted in the center comes out clean (see Note). Serve immediately with a spoon.

Note: Cooking times will vary depending on the power of your microwave. Continue microwaving the cookie in 15-second intervals, if necessary.

PER SERVING: CALORIES 583 FAT 35g PROTEIN 7g CARB 64g FIBER 2g CHOL 247mg IRON 3mg SODIUM 312mg CALC 106mg

This is my version of the Pizookie® from BJ's Restaurant & Brewhouse. The warm freshly-baked cookie skillet topped with ice cream is so simple yet so good that I had to be able to have it at home. And you can't beat the delicious cookie smell when it comes out of the oven.

BROWN BUTTER CHOCOLATE CHIP SKILLET

SERVES 6   PREP TIME: 15 MINUTES   TOTAL TIME: 30 MINUTES   KF VEG

1 ¾ cups all-purpose flour

½ teaspoon baking soda

½ teaspoon salt

14 tablespoons unsalted butter

⅓ cup granulated sugar

½ cup packed dark brown sugar

2 teaspoons vanilla extract

1 large egg

1 large egg yolk

1 cup chocolate chips

Ice cream, for serving, optional

Caramel sauce, for serving, optional

1. Preheat the oven to 375°F. Lightly coat two 5-inch cast-iron skillets with nonstick spray.

2. In a large bowl, combine the flour, baking soda, and salt; set aside.

3. Melt 10 tablespoons butter in a medium saucepan over medium heat. Cook, whisking constantly, until the butter begins to turn a golden brown, about 3 minutes. Remove from heat; strain through a cheesecloth or fine sieve.

4. Stir in the remaining 4 tablespoons butter until completely melted. Whisk in the sugars and vanilla until well combined. Whisk in the egg and egg yolk until well combined. Add the flour mixture, beating just until incorporated. Gently fold in the chocolate chips.

5. Divide the mixture into the prepared skillets. Bake until the edges are golden brown but the center is still moist, 12 to 15 minutes.

6. Serve immediately, topped with ice cream and drizzled with caramel sauce, if desired.

PER SERVING: CALORIES 633 FAT 37.2g PROTEIN 6g CARB 73g FIBER 3g CHOL 133mg IRON 3mg SODIUM 320mg CALC 31mg

These bad boys are perfect for any special occasion from birthdays to holidays. They are irresistible bite-sized cheesecakes for crying out loud! They also make for easy serving and portion control (for some, definitely not for me). If you don't have a mini cheesecake pan, a muffin tin will also work just fine.

MINI VANILLA BEAN TURTLE CHEESECAKES

MAKES 12   **PREP TIME:** 20 MINUTES   **TOTAL TIME:** 35 MINUTES, PLUS CHILLING   `KF` `VEG`

⅔ cup graham cracker crumbs

2 tablespoons unsalted butter, melted

2 (8-ounce) packages cream cheese, softened

½ cup sugar

2 large eggs

½ teaspoon vanilla extract

1 vanilla bean, split in half lengthwise and seeds scraped and reserved

¼ cup caramel sauce

¼ cup chocolate chips, melted

12 pecan halves, for garnish

1. Preheat the oven to 325°F. Lightly oil a mini cheesecake pan, or coat it with nonstick spray.

2. In a small bowl, combine the graham cracker crumbs and melted butter until a crumbly, moist mixture forms. Press 1 tablespoon of the crumb mixture into the bottom of each prepared cup; set aside.

3. In the bowl of an electric mixer fitted with the paddle attachment, beat the cream cheese and sugar until smooth, scraping the sides of the bowl and beaters as needed. Beat in the eggs, one at a time, until well combined. Beat in the vanilla and vanilla bean seeds until well combined.

4. Divide the filling evenly among the cups.

5. Bake until centers are almost set, 13 to 15 minutes. Let cool, and refrigerate for at least 2 hours.

6. Serve chilled, drizzled with caramel, melted chocolate, and pecan halves.

PER SERVING: CALORIES 271 **FAT** 19.5g **PROTEIN** 4g **CARB** 21g **FIBER** 1g **CHOL** 78mg **IRON** 1mg **SODIUM** 186mg **CALC** 49mg

I know, it's impossible to say no to those adorable Girl Scouts when they set up shop and sell their cookies. But even those girls can't offer you this—a buttery donut with all the flavors of the Samoa cookies, with salted caramel, toasted coconut flakes, and melted chocolate. It's perfection, really.

MINI SAMOA DONUTS

MAKES 12　**PREP TIME:** 25 MINUTES　**TOTAL TIME:** 30 MINUTES　`KF` `VEG`

¾ cup all-purpose flour

⅓ cup sugar

2 tablespoons cornstarch

1 teaspoon baking powder

½ teaspoon salt

⅓ cup plus 2 tablespoons milk

1 ½ teaspoons white vinegar

1 tablespoon unsalted butter, melted

1 large egg

FOR THE TOPPINGS

¼ cup salted caramel

½ cup unsweetened coconut flakes, toasted

½ cup semi-sweet chocolate chips, melted

1. Preheat the oven to 425°F. Lightly oil a mini donut pan, or coat it with nonstick spray.

2. In a large bowl, combine the flour, sugar, cornstarch, baking powder, and salt.

3. In a small bowl, whisk together the milk, vinegar, butter, and egg. Pour it over the dry ingredients, and stir using a rubber spatula just until moist.

4. Scoop the batter evenly into the donut pan. Bake for 4 to 5 minutes, or until the donuts are slightly browned and spring back when touched.

5. Let the donuts cool for 10 minutes, and dip the tops into the salted caramel. Sprinkle with toasted coconut flakes, and drizzle with chocolate.

6. Allow the chocolate to set before serving.

PER SERVING: CALORIES 139 **FAT** 5.1g **PROTEIN** 2g **CARB** 22g **FIBER** 1g **CHOL** 19mg **IRON** 1mg **SODIUM** 168mg **CALC** 40mg

METRIC EQUIVALENTS

The information in the following charts is provided to help cooks outside the United States successfully use the recipes in this book. All equivalents are approximate.

COOKING TEMPERATURES

FAHRENHEIT	CELSIUS
32° F	0° C
68° F	20° C
212° F	100° C
325° F	160° C
350° F	180° C
375° F	190° C
400° F	200° C
425° F	220° C
450° F	230° C

DRY INGREDIENTS BY WEIGHT

(To convert ounces to grams, multiply the number of ounces by 30.)

1 oz	=	$\frac{1}{16}$ lb	=	30 g
4 oz	=	$\frac{1}{4}$ lb	=	120 g
8 oz	=	$\frac{1}{2}$ lb	=	240 g
12 oz	=	$\frac{3}{4}$ lb	=	360 g
16 oz	=	1 lb	=	480 g

LIQUID INGREDIENTS BY VOLUME

$\frac{1}{4}$ tsp =				1 ml
$\frac{1}{2}$ tsp =				2 ml
1 tsp =				5 ml
3 tsp =	1 Tbsp =		$\frac{1}{2}$ fl oz =	15 ml
	2 Tbsp =	$\frac{1}{8}$ cup =	1 fl oz =	30 ml
	4 Tbsp =	$\frac{1}{4}$ cup =	2 fl oz =	60 ml
	5 $\frac{1}{3}$ Tbsp =	$\frac{1}{3}$ cup =	3 fl oz =	80 ml
	8 Tbsp =	$\frac{1}{2}$ cup =	4 fl oz =	120 ml
	10 $\frac{2}{3}$ Tbsp =	$\frac{2}{3}$ cup =	5 fl oz =	160 ml
	12 Tbsp =	$\frac{3}{4}$ cup =	6 fl oz =	180 ml
	16 Tbsp =	1 cup =	8 fl oz =	240 ml
	1 pt =	2 cups =	16 fl oz =	480 ml
	1 qt =	4 cups =	32 fl oz =	960 ml
			33 fl oz =	1000 ml = 1 l

Special Offer!

As a thank you for purchasing this cookbook, my friends at Peapod are offering a special promotion to Damn Delicious readers.

Enjoy the convenience of grocery delivery to your home or office. Enter the promotional code to save **$20** on your first Peapod order of $60 or more.

peapod.com

CODE:

DMNDLCS

Limit one offer per household. Cannot be combined with any other offer. Offer excludes alcoholic beverages, gift cards, postage stamps and any other purchase prohibited by law. Peapod is not available in all locations. Expires 12/31/2017.

ACKNOWLEDGMENTS

This cookbook came about with the help of so many people.

To my one and only editor, Betty Wong. I'm pretty sure I'm right when I say you may just be the most patient editor of all time. Despite my pushing deadlines, making about 1,849,294 recipe revisions, shooting only macro when told otherwise, last minute cancellations and all, you have truly been amazing and managed to accommodate everything that has unfolded during this two-year journey. At one point, I was almost ready to throw in the towel, but you helped me finish this book the way it was meant to be, and that is something I will always take with me.

To the entire Oxmoor House and Time Inc. Books team, thank you for all the hard work.

To Maria Ribas, I'm never going to forget that first e-mail from you. I thought it was spam. A joke. But something in my gut told me to take that phone call with you. The minute we started talking, I knew this project was happening. And in all honesty, this book would never have begun without you. Thank you for believing in me and encouraging me to do this. I'm so glad I did. You've made a dream become a reality. Thanks also to the Howard Morhaim Agency.

To Trever Hoehne, Kyle Estudillo, Anthony Merante, Marian Cooper Cairns, Arno Diem, Camille Carter, Thayer Gowdy, Karen Schaupeter, Felicity Keane, Maribeth Jones, Iain Bagwell, and Celine Russell: Thank you all for being so patient with me during the book's photoshoots. I am not very comfortable in front of a camera, but you guys are all rock stars for making it work—even when that meant dealing with two crazy corgis in a tiny apartment or shooting outdoors on a rainy day!

To Danica Buenaventura. We've been through so much these past 10 years. (Maybe a little too much if you factor in the whole Jack Bauer-Spain phase.) Thanks for always being there for me through thick and thin, for taking home leftovers to your family, for taste-testing, and for always returning my Tupperware. It's really just the Tupperware that I'm grateful for.

To Laura Stace. You make me feel sane even when I'm doing the craziest things, and you always look out for me, no matter what. Thanks for believing in me and for making me believe in myself. You're like the big sister I've never had, but always wanted.

To Ronnica Choi. You've seen everything since we were 12 years old. The good, the bad, the laughter, the tears. All of it. Thanks for always having my back and supporting me through all of this. You know we'll always have Kettleman City as our safety.

And to Nick Hounslow. Where do I even start? It's been a whirlwind of a year and I'm incredibly grateful to be going through this whole new chapter with you as part of my life. You've somehow kept me grounded during my meltdowns (it might be the British accent) and pushed me to go outside my limits. You're always somehow right too—which is annoying by the way. But seriously, thank you for just being in my life.

#damndeliciouscookbook

INDEX

G

H

K